PRESENTED TO:

FROM:

DATE:

THE YEAR of LIVING HAPPY

Contented and Connected
in a Crazy World

ALLI WORTHINGTON

ZONDERVAN

The Year of Living Happy

Copyright © 2018 by Alli Worthington

This title is also available as a Zondervan ebook.

Requests for information should be addressed to:
Zondervan, 3900 Sparks Dr. SE, Grand Rapids, Michigan 49546

Library of Congress Cataloging-in-Publication Data

ISBN 978-0-310-09489-0

Published in association with literary agent Jenni Burke of D. C. Jacobson & Associates LLC, an Author Management Company. www.dcjacobson.com.

Art direction: Adam Hill
Interior design: Mallory Collins

Printed in China

18 19 20 21 22 DSC 10 9 8 7 6 5 4 3 2 1

CONTENTS

PART 6: HAPPY IN A WORLD OF CRAZY

PART 7: WHEN HAPPINESS IS HARD

PART 8: HEALTHY-HAPPY-WHOLE

PART 9: CHOOSING HAPPINESS

PART 10: THE POWER OF HAPPY WORDS

PART 11: A HAPPY HEART IS GOOD MEDICINE

PART 12: BUILDING A HAPPY LIFE

A NOTE FROM ALLI

Dear Friend,

The fact that you are set to embark upon this happiness journey absolutely thrills me! I believe that as women of God, we are called to be beacons of light, hope, and yes, *happiness* in this dark world. The world needs us to share the gospel and do it with great happiness.

I used to believe the search for happiness was a superficial pursuit, that happiness and holiness were mutually exclusive. But now I understand they go hand in hand. This work of seeking authentic happiness is important, and it is holy. As we seek after the things that create real happiness in us, we find God. And when we live the life God has created us to live, securely and obediently trusting Him in all areas, we are happier.

Deep joy and a happy life are not dependent upon our day-to-day life events, and they are not superficial. As we seek the Lord and delight in all that He has for us (no matter our circumstances), we not only change, but we begin to change everyone who comes in contact with us.

My hope for *The Year of Living Happy* is to bring the truth of Scripture and best of modern research together as a guide to real happiness.

I've collected all my favorite and most helpful insights, research, and truths as a road map for you as you embark on the important work of choosing happiness in your life.

As women of God, let's be the ones who fight for authentic happiness and teach our families, our friends, and our communities by our example.

As we begin this happiness journey together, I pray you will discover new truths, find some amazing life hacks, and have your eyes opened to the importance of holy happiness.

All my love,

Alli

1

MADE TO BE HAPPY

You were created to experience joy!

HAPPY ROOTS

I have a sweet friend who always says, "Girl, my happy has deep roots."

Regardless of her life circumstances, good or bad, she reminds me that her happiness is rooted way past the temporary trials of the day to the eternal goodness of God. I am always amazed at the way she responds to what life throws at her; whether it's burned casseroles or broken bones, she calmly, joyfully takes it in stride.

I love my friend's expression because it reminds me that happiness is something God wants for me. It's okay for me to desire happiness because it's God's desire for me as well.

It's also a great reminder that God wants us to stay rooted in Him to have happy, full lives that bear wonderful fruit. As Christians, we are allowed to be happy; we just need to keep in mind that true happiness comes only from Him. It does not come through our material possessions, our relationships, or our circumstances.

When our happy has deep roots, those roots allow us to weather the droughts and storms of life. They allow us to trust in the goodness of God and to produce sweet fruit that reflects the heart of our loving

Savior, Jesus. Jeremiah 17 tells us, "Blessed is the man who trusts in the LORD and whose trust is the LORD. For he will be like a tree planted by the water, that extends its roots by a stream and will not fear when the heat comes; but its leaves will be green, and it will not be anxious in a year of drought nor cease to yield fruit" (vv. 7–8 NASB). In short, our deep roots allow us to live happy lives.

My prayer for you today is that your happy will have deep roots. And my prayer for you this year is that your roots will grow so deep toward the eternal goodness of God that you will be forever changed.

Today, open your Bible to Jeremiah 17:7-8, record the date there or below, and write the phrase, "My happy has deep roots." Consider doodling or drawing around the phrase to help it go even deeper into your brain.[1]

_____

_____

_____

HAPPINESS IS A WORTHY GOAL

Growing up, I remember being told that joy was spelled, "J-O-Y"—Jesus, others, and you. It was supposed to be a reminder that joy comes from having the right priorities, and that's certainly true. But it seemed as if joy were always pitted against happiness. While joy was godly and spiritual, happiness was shallow and selfish. But as I kept walking with Jesus, I came to understand that seeking to follow God and seeking to be happy weren't mutually exclusive.

Our happiness (and our joy) are tied to what we desire most. Our problem with seeking happiness is that we try to find it in things that can't sustain our happiness. But when we desire to find our happiness in God, we access a well of joy that won't run dry.

Scripture tells us, "Take delight in the LORD, and he will give you the desires of your heart" (Psalm 37:4). I used to think that meant God would give me whatever I wanted if I seemed happy enough to Him. Now I've come to see that when my happiness is placed securely in God, He will be the desire of my heart. And when He's the desire of my heart, my happiness isn't going anywhere.

God designed us to seek happiness in Him and to want to have the source of our happiness be in Him. As John Piper said, "God is most glorified in you when you are most satisfied in him."[1]

Think about your ideas of happiness. Have you given yourself permission to be happy? Pray and ask the Lord to help you find your happiness in Him and to live according to His laws. Record any thoughts you have or insights He gives you.

_____

_____

_____

_____

_____

_____

_____

APPRECIATING HOW UNIQUELY WE ARE CREATED

I once heard it said that if we knew who God created us to be, we would never want to act like anyone else. We would celebrate even the things we may feel insecure about. We would see ourselves as God sees us. We wouldn't see our quirks as flaws, but would begin to see them as part of the unique blueprint God used when He made us.

Sometimes it's so easy to be unappreciative of God's unique design for us, especially when we begin to compare our design with others'. Doesn't God know we'd be so much happier if we were slightly more proportional, or maybe more artistic, or possibly less afraid of public speaking? Yet, in all our unique variations, God has given each of us a unique way to live a life that glorifies Him.

Allow yourself to be the unique person God created you to be, and surround yourself with those who love you for who you really are. Allow yourself the freedom that comes from not having to live up to other people's expectations of how your life should be.

One of the most common regrets people have at the end of their lives is, "I wish I'd had the courage to live a life true to myself, not the life others expected of me." We can rest in the knowledge that God knew exactly what He was doing when He knit each of us together. Learn to express to Him, "I praise you because I am fearfully and wonderfully made; your works are wonderful, I know that full well" (Psalm 139:14).

List as many unique qualities about yourself as you can think of . . . yes, every single one. Thank God for each and every one you list. Thank Him that you are fearfully and wonderfully made. Embracing your uniqueness teaches you to be happy just as you are.

_____

_____

_____

_____

_____

_____

CREATED FOR CREATIVITY

W hen I first had the idea that I wanted to write a book, I was thrilled and terrified all at the same time. On one hand, I was excited at the prospect of getting to create something that could benefit others. On the other hand, however, when I thought about the fact that people were going to actually read my work, it seemed scary and overwhelming. What if they didn't agree with me? What if they thought I was a terrible writer? The idea of setting myself up for that kind of judgment was almost more than I could handle.

It was like being on the high dive and making the decision to either jump or make the humble climb back down to more comfortable heights. One option was full of uncertainty and possibility, while the other was safe and sure.

Maybe you've been there too—afraid to take the plunge but unwilling to climb back down the ladder.

In those moments when our fears keep us paralyzed in uncertainty, let's remember that our Creator has made us in His creative image. The book of Exodus reminds us, "He has filled [us] with the Spirit of God, with wisdom, with understanding, with knowledge and with all kinds of skills" (35:31). We were made to make things, innovate, and exercise the unique gifts God has impressed upon us.

Today, do something creative. Paint, write a poem,
draw, knit; do what your heart dreams of doing.
Then take a risk and show it to someone!

_____

_____

_____

_____

_____

_____

_____

_____

TAKE A STEP TOWARD YOUR PASSION

Remember when you were just starting out in life? Back then, it seemed life was presenting you with limitless opportunities and possibilities. But now, maybe it feels as if you've already made your big life choices and you might've missed your window of opportunity.

Let me assure you, it is never too late to start something new.[1]

How do I know? I know because history is filled with so many examples of people who stepped into their passion later in their lives. Benjamin Franklin discovered the properties of electricity when he was forty.[2] Julia Child made her debut TV appearance at fifty-one.[3] And J. R. R. Tolkien published *The Lord of the Rings* when he was sixty-two.[4]

Then there was Abraham. Abraham was seventy-five years old when God called him to go to the land of Canaan and promised him offspring, while his wife, Sarah, was not much younger. They had spent years dreaming of what it would be like to have a family and then God promised them children at the ripe old ages of seventy-five and sixty-five, but He didn't give them their firstborn until Abraham was a hundred and Sarah was ninety!

Think about what it would be like to have a promise from God that wouldn't be fulfilled until twenty-five years later. Still, Abraham spent each and every day taking one step after the other toward the promises God had for him. Abraham understood what the psalmist meant when he said, "The LORD makes firm the steps of the one who delights in him" (37:23).

If we can learn one thing from Abraham, it's that God has adventure for you in every season of life. He created you to know Him, love Him, and find your fulfillment (and happiness) in following the passions and dreams He's given you. It's never too late to take your next step.

Is there a dream you've had for a while, but you've been afraid to take a step toward achieving it? Maybe it's a big dream; maybe it's a small dream. Whatever it is, write that dream here. Then write what you think your life might look like when that dream becomes a reality.

I don't know what my dream is I want to write words that matter

WHAT ARE YOUR GREEN PASTURES?

Everyone recharges differently. Personally, I love to sing worship songs, snuggle up with my family and watch movies, and read inspirational books. This is my version of lying in green pastures.

When life has me wound up too tightly, I know I can always unwind and recharge through these activities. In these small moments, when I reconnect with God and others, I feel a steady stream of peace (and happiness) fill my life.

In the Psalms, David talks about God as a shepherd who leads him to peace. David says, "He makes me lie down in green pastures, he leads me beside quiet waters, he refreshes my soul" (Psalm 23:2–3).

To be honest, I'm glad the things David mentions here aren't quite literal. (Give me my creature comforts any day over bug bites and sunscreen!) Yet, at the heart of what David's saying is an awareness of God's desire for him to find moments of peace, rest, and happiness in his Shepherd.

God has made us all so differently, which means we all have our own green pastures. For some, it's naps in the hammock in the backyard.

For others, it's a quiet night in with a book. Maybe for you, it's a big, loud dinner with good friends. For all of us, it's taking advantage of the moments when God leads us to where we can drink deeply of His goodness.

So what are your green pastures? Has it been so long since you've allowed yourself to simply rest that maybe you don't even remember? Ask yourself this question: *What leaves me feeling full, peaceful, and happy?* Today, be intentional about lying down in your green pastures and let your soul be refreshed.

_____

_____

_____

_____

_____

THE IMPORTANCE OF GUARDRAILS

I was driving along the coast of California recently—white-knuckling that steering wheel like nobody's business! You see, some parts of the coast of California are quite hilly, with deadly drop-offs around hairpin turns that follow the curve of the ocean. It's scary in the daytime, but at night, it's terrifying. (Did I mention the sun was setting?)

Were it not for the guardrails all along the edge of that highway, the road would be treacherous and unforgiving to even the smallest mistakes.

You know the funny thing about guardrails? Most of us don't pay them any mind until we need them. I've never heard anyone say, "You know what I hate when I'm driving? I hate guardrails. They're the worst!" Nope. Not one person has ever complained to me about a guardrail. In fact, the only time I have ever heard someone talk about a guardrail at all was when one saved her life.

However, when someone brings up the idea of having guardrails in other areas of our lives, we're often surprised at the thought. Be it guardrails for our marriage, our kids, our career, or our schedule, the idea that our freedom might be hampered by some kind of restraint is a hard pill to swallow for many of us.

But just as guardrails keep us from disaster on the road, the guardrails that God gives us keep us from disaster in our lives. God, in His wisdom, sets guardrails along our path to keep us focused, dependent on Him, and moving in the right direction toward the life we were created to live. Even before we took our first breath, God established these boundaries for our good. The book of Psalms tells us, "Your eyes saw my unformed body; all the days ordained for me were written in your book before one of them came to be" (139:16). Though these guardrails might seem as if they're keeping us from what we think will make us happy, God knows that without them we would never know the happy life He has planned for us.

His guardrails are for our good—to keep us securely in the center of His will, which not surprisingly is also where our happiness is rooted.

Today, ask yourself, where have you seen God place guardrails in your life? How did those guardrails keep you from disaster?

_____

_____

A MEEK SPIRIT

I used to think having a meek spirit meant I needed to be boring. A meek spirit meant I didn't intentionally rock the boat by saying something that could offend anyone. It meant I didn't speak up or speak out, so for me, I rarely spoke at all. Trust me, I took the whole, "gentle and quiet spirit" thing very seriously. As best as I could tell, a meek spirit meant living an exceptionally boring Christian life.

It was only later that a mentor explained to me that I was wrongly interpreting 1 Peter 3:4, which says, "Rather, it should be that of your inner self, the unfading beauty of a gentle and quit spirit, which is of great worth in God's sight." She said, "Alli, you've confused having a gentle and quiet spirit with having a gentle and quiet personality."

For many of us, this definition flies in the face of the image that pops into our minds when we think of having a meek spirit. But God made us who we are for a reason.

From my mentor I learned that meekness means being powerful not in ourselves, but in God. If our power finds its source in the strength of the Savior, seeking to serve others and not dominate them, then we are living the powerful Christian life we are meant to live.

I believe we are our happiest selves when we are living life in the personality that God gave us. Today, boldly be who God made you to be! He wants you to powerfully live out the purpose He's given you.

Meek women are strong women who find their strength in God!

> What comes into your mind when you think of a "meek Christian woman"? Ask the Lord to reveal to you the truth of what it means to powerfully live out the purpose He's given you.
>
> _____
>
> _____
>
> _____
>
> _____
>
> _____

REFLECTION

2

HOLINESS IS HAPPINESS

When your goal is holiness, happiness can follow.

DON'T LET PRIDE POISON YOUR HAPPINESS

In the months following the release of *Breaking Busy*, I was floored by how well it was received and all the incredibly nice things people had to say about the book. The whole experience was like something out of a dream. The fact that I had written and published a book was crazy enough, and then to learn that so many people were finding the book helpful and encouraging was more than I could have ever expected.

But, like anything else, the book wasn't for everyone, and not everyone thought it was absolutely amazing. And to be perfectly transparent, the criticism got to me. It really got to me. I swung from feeling completely humbled that someone read—and was helped by—my book to feeling threatened and humiliated when someone didn't like my work.

After the thrill of positive reviews, the criticisms stoked my pride and absolutely poisoned my happiness. So when someone left me a negative review, Pride said, "Alli, those people apparently don't realize how much the book could help them. Clearly they don't get it."

Pride whispers lies that we deserve something better, that we are above other people, and, worst of all, that we are owed their praise. Pride sits on our shoulder and tells us we should have more. And let me tell you, my pride got the best of me that time around!

But in His gentleness, the Lord spoke this truth over me from Proverbs 11:2: "When pride comes, then comes disgrace, but with humility comes wisdom." It was humbling for me to admit that pride had gotten the best of me. But recognizing it, and then asking the Lord to help me be humble, actually helped me learn to be content whether the reviews were good or bad.

Pride poisons our ability to know the happiness that comes from being content. But humility is the soil where happiness grows. It allows us to be filled with gratitude at the wonder of God's goodness in our lives.

Ask God to humble you and show you where your pride has poisoned your happiness. Because humility is the soil where happiness grows, plant some seeds and watch your year of happiness flourish!

_____

_____

GOD IS ALWAYS ON YOUR SIDE

I seem to suffer from short-term memory loss when it comes to remembering God's faithfulness in my life. Despite the countless times that I've agonized over my circumstances, waited on Him to move, and watched in utter amazement as He's provided for me time and time again, when life seems unsteady my first response isn't typically to trust God, but instead to question what He's up to.

Do you experience this too? When our little world is rocked, we are so quick to point to the wind and waves but disregard the One who speaks peace to both? It's so easy to forget that God is with us, that He is for us, and that He has, is, and will always work all things together for our good.

In Romans 8:28, the apostle Paul says, "We know that in all things God works for the good of those who love him, who have been called according to his purpose." This means that despite what our present circumstances might say to us and despite the anxiety of our own hearts, our God is with us and is for us. I don't know about you, but this makes me want to go walk on some water!

Even when it feels as if our lives are so far removed from His purposes, nothing is outside His reach. Our God remains faithful to us.

Spend some time today thanking God for His good purposes in you. As you pray, record times you can recall His faithfulness to you.

_____

_____

_____

_____

_____

_____

_____

_____

BREAKFAST WITH JESUS

Peter is my favorite disciple because of how obviously flawed and human he is. (Man, can I relate to Peter!) After he denied knowing Jesus three times, he was completely (and pretty understandably) devastated. Believing his time as a disciple was over, he returned to his previous way of life as a fisherman. (Isn't that like all of us? When we feel lost, we return so quickly to our old ways. But even when we do, God continues to come after us!)

As Peter sat in his boat, along with the other disciples, he felt lost. Not only had he failed to come to the aid of Jesus when He needed him most, now Peter couldn't even catch fish! He'd been fishing all night and had nothing to show for it.

Then from the shore, a man tells them to cast their net to the other side of the boat. They did cast their net on the other side of the boat and caught 153 fish.

John, who was with Peter on the boat, announced it was the Lord on the shore, and Peter leapt into the water to find his way back to Jesus. Peter didn't stay stuck in his own failures on that boat. He wasn't going to waste another minute finding his way back into Jesus' arms.

By the time Peter reached Jesus on the shore, I'm sure he expected Jesus to let him have it. Instead, he found Jesus ready to receive him back into His grace—and with a hot breakfast to top it off!

How often do we do this in our own lives? We are so quick to replace the grace-filled words of Jesus with the condemnation we feel we should get for our mistakes. We forget that because of Jesus there is no longer any condemnation left for us! Jesus received our punishment so we could instead receive His love. Romans 8:1 affirms this for us: "There is now no condemnation for those who are in Christ Jesus."

Jesus is there to receive us back from our mistakes. He stands on the shore ready to love us!

Think about an occasion when you spent time beating yourself up over a mistake. Now imagine what Jesus would say to you. Write yourself a letter from Him in which He tells you how He feels about you. Remember, just like with Peter, Jesus isn't there to condemn you but to love you.

_____

_____

DIVINE PROTECTION

Can you imagine what it would've been like in the garden of Eden? Picture for a moment how incredible your quiet time would be if it consisted of actually walking with God in the cool of the day. Not only that, but your world would have been completely at peace and lacking nothing—always getting to enjoy the best of the best.

If we were to experience true happiness from living with God in the garden, you think it'd be pretty easy not to do the one thing God said would ruin it, right?

But we know that's not how the story ended. The Serpent convinced Adam and Eve of the most basic and insidious lie: God's rules keep us from being happy.

By twisting the words of God, the Serpent persuaded our ancient grandparents to believe that God was keeping true happiness from them.

The Enemy isn't all that creative and hasn't changed his tactics on us. He still uses the same, tired argument that God's rules are meant to rob us of our happiness because we buy it so readily. By stroking our egos, he convinces us that we know how to make ourselves happy far better than our Maker does.

God's commandments are actually designed to keep us happy. Proverbs tells us, "Whoever gives heed to instruction prospers, and blessed is the one who trusts in the LORD" (16:20).

When we learn to faithfully follow the instructions God has given us in His Word, we will find that our lives end up looking a lot more like the garden He intended for us.

Today, spend some time with the Lord asking Him to show you the ways in which you've tried to make yourself happy instead of faithfully following His instruction. Draw two columns on the Reflection page at the end of this section or in the pages of your journal. On one side write, "Ways I have tried to make myself happy." On the other side write, "Is it working?" And then put a check mark by those things you have been doing that *truly* bring happiness to your life.

_____

_____

_____

I AM WITH YOU

I've always thought that if God were physically with me I would be able to trust Him in any circumstance. It makes sense that if I could just see Him, His presence alone would be comforting enough to get me through anything that came my way.

The Israelites had that experience. After they were freed from slavery in Egypt, God led them through the wilderness as a pillar of cloud by day and a pillar of fire by night. They always knew He was there. They didn't just feel His presence, they saw a physical representation of His glory as they took each step.

However, even though they had God leading them by the hand, the Israelites still needed faith to trust that where He was taking them was for their good.

In John 16:7, Jesus says that He's given us something better than His physical self when He says, "Very truly I tell you, it is for your good that I am going away. Unless I go away, the Advocate will not come to you; but if I go, I will send him to you."

The Advocate Jesus is talking about is the Holy Spirit. We now have the very presence of God within us, and He leads us to His truth and helps us walk in His way.

Our God is always with us, amid every moment of life, constantly leading us to the promises He has for us. Trust that where He's taking you is for your good!

Think about what it means to have the Holy Spirit of God living inside of you. Answer the following questions here or in the pages of your journal: What does it mean to you that the Spirit of God lives in you? What does that look like lived out each day?

_____

_____

_____

_____

_____

STARTING YOUR DAY WITH JOY (HAPPINESS INSURANCE)

My best days are the ones when I wake up ready to spend time with Jesus, because I know that when I do, I'm starting my day off with joy.

On the days when I don't start my morning with Him, it shows. When we are together, He reminds me who I am, what He's created me for, and the love He's shown to me and others. Without that time, it isn't long until my happy-meter runs down to zero. That's because God created us so that we would find our happiness in Him and Him alone!

For me to be truly happy, no matter what unpredictable things are happening in my world, I have to take the time to sit with Jesus, the source of all happiness.

So often we're like the woman at the well, looking for our happiness in so many other places, even though the very source of happiness is sitting right in front of us. In those moments, Jesus looks at us with grace in His eyes and says, "If you knew the gift of God and who it is that asks you for a drink, you would have asked him and he would have given you living water" (John 4:10).

When we start our day with Jesus, we're starting it with the very source of all happiness.

What does your daily time with the Lord look like? Commit yourself to spending time with Jesus at the start of every day, even if it's only five minutes, and watch as you're filled up with the happiness that only comes from Him! If this is a new commitment, or a commitment you want to renew, write it down here or in your journal. Be specific about when, where, and how you will spend your time with the Lord each day.

_____

_____

_____

_____

_____

TRUST HIS TIMING

Imagine God had promised to give you the one thing you desired more than anything. Now imagine it taking twenty-five years to accomplish, and imagine being seventy-five when God made the promise to you. This is what happened to Abraham. God had promised Abraham and his wife, Sarah, that they would be given a son who would be the first of a line of descendants that would outnumber the stars in the sky. This was no doubt a promise that was hard to believe at year one, much less at year twenty-five!

After ten years of waiting for God to fulfill His promise, Abraham and Sarah took matters into their own hands with disastrous results. (Anyone else out there ever done this? Taken matters into your own hands instead of waiting on God's timing? Dated the wrong guy because you thought God wasn't going to provide one? Took the wrong job because you worried He might not come through in time for you to pay your bills? I get it y'all. Waiting is hard work!)

Instead of waiting for God to provide what He had promised, Abraham and Sarah figured they would help God out, so they found a shortcut. And it wasn't long before this shortcut blew up in their faces. Instead of waiting for the blessing God had designed, they introduced resentment and heartache into their lives. They thought they knew better, but God always knows best.

I've heard many people say, "God is never early, and He's never late. He's always right on time." We might know this, but we're still not great at waiting. When impatience threatens to steal our happiness, we have to remind ourselves to make the decision to trust His timing.

What is something you have been waiting on God to bring to fruition? How has this affected your trust in God? Write on a note card, "I can trust God's timing." Now place that note card somewhere you will see it regularly. Each time you see it, pray, saying, "Thank You, God. I know Your perfect timing is for my good. And I trust You."

_____

_____

_____

CLOTHING OURSELVES WITH GOOD

Now that I'm past forty, I keep seeing articles that tell me how to dress my age. (And they call forty middle-aged, but let's not get into that ridiculousness. I still feel seventeen!) Honestly, I spend a lot of time trying to figure out how to dress myself well.

Skinny jeans, ripped jeans, mom jeans . . . I'm never sure what the latest trends are these days. But one of the things that has definitely improved with age is the realization that the importance of what I wear on the outside pales in comparison to how I'm clothed on the inside.

I love what Paul says in Colossians 3:12, "As God's chosen people, holy and dearly loved, clothe yourselves with compassion, kindness, humility, gentleness and patience."

In other words, show on the outside what God has done on the inside, not with colors and patterns, but with compassion and patience. Imagine the joy we would feel if we were wrapped up in the holy and beloved identity we've received as God's people!

To live as people who are holy and dearly loved, we have to take off the old clothes we're so used to wearing. We have to exchange our indifference for His compassion, our selfishness for His kindness, our pride for His humility, our harsh nature for His gentle ways, and our restlessness for His patience. We have to walk in the truth of what it means to be His people!

Friend, what "old clothes" are you hanging onto that you need to exchange for God's new clothes? Write those here or in your journal. What do God's new clothes look like? God has covered us with His grace, so let's show on the outside what He's already done on the inside!

_____

_____

_____

_____

_____

_____

GIRD YOUR LOINS

In the movie *The Devil Wears Prada*, when Meryl Streep is about to walk into the office, her longtime assistant yells, "Gird your loins!" I always laugh at that scene, even though I had no idea what that phrase actually meant until recently. Naturally, I Googled the phrase and was quite surprised (and a little bit tickled) by what it meant.

Long ago, people (male people) used to wear long flowy tunics with nothing under them (nothing covering their "loins," if you will). When they were preparing to do any kind of work, but especially when they were going to go into battle, they literally had to tuck the long pieces of fabric up around their waist, then between their legs in order to "secure themselves," if you know what I mean. It kind of makes me giggle because it looks like a makeshift diaper.

Over time, *gird your loins* came to mean, "protect yourself, or prepare for the incoming assault." In Ephesians 6, where Paul is talking about the armor of God, some translations tell you to gird your loins "with the belt of truth buckled around your waist, with the breastplate of righteousness in place" (v. 14). Basically, we are told to protect ourselves with truth to prepare for the battle we will face (with our Enemy) by literally wrapping ourselves in truth.

The truth Paul is talking about is God's Word. Reading it allows us to see truth. Writing it allows us to remember truth. And memorizing it allows us to wear truth. The Word of God is the most protective piece of armor we can wear into the daily battles of our lives.

Choose a favorite verse in the Bible, perhaps one that has a special meaning in your life. Write it out. Now step into your creative mind and draw or paint a picture that symbolizes this verse to you. And lastly, memorize the verse so you can wrap yourself in the truth of it as you gird your loins!

_____

_____

_____

_____

GOD'S PLAN, NOT MY PLAN

As a business coach and strategist, I love developing plans. Plans are the chocolate to my peanut butter. They are the icing to my cake. They are the pepperoni to my pizza. (Have you noticed all my analogies are food related?) My point is: I love plans. (And snacks.)

Once I map out a plan, I'm not a fan of anyone telling me to change my direction. I'm very decisive like that. But God, in His infinite wisdom and desire to keep me humble, has taken so many of my brilliant plans and rerouted them in a completely different direction.

I once built a news website that I quickly realized I had no desire to run.

I built an app that no one ever even wanted.

Friend, I have stories and stories of my failed entrepreneurial ideas!

There have been times when I have fought God on these plans tooth and nail (which is Southern for "kicking and screaming"). And you know how I felt when I was resisting His leading? Miserable.

I have had to learn to turn over the reins and the strategic plans of my life to God. And in the process, I have learned that although His ways are not my ways, His plans are always infinitely better than my own.

Only God knows what will truly make us happy. Only God can fill the deepest desires of our hearts. His Word reminds us, "Oh, the depth of the riches of the wisdom and knowledge of God! How unsearchable his judgments, and his paths beyond tracing out!" (Romans 11:33). You can trust Him to direct, plan, and lead your life. That is where real happiness comes from.

Have you sensed that God has a different path for your life than the one you are on? If so, stop right now and ask Him how to follow His lead. Record what you sense Him leading you to do. Then take the steps He's calling you to take.

_____

_____

_____

_____

_____

_____

REFLECTION

3

HAPPINESS IN THE HERE AND NOW

You can learn to be happy right where you are.

STAYING MINDFUL

By nature, I focus on the future. Being in the moment has always been a challenge for me because I love dreaming big about future possibilities. I love the rush of excitement that comes from thinking about new goals and all the what-ifs that go along with them.

One cool, spring afternoon I stood looking out the window and said to myself, *I can't wait until the weather warms up a bit. When it gets warmer, I'm going to spend some time sitting outside, enjoying the sunshine, and reading a good book.* Right about that time, Mollie, our golden retriever, nudged me to let her outside. I opened the door and watched as she barreled past me and literally frolicked in the field just beyond our backyard.

She didn't need a future set of circumstances to enjoy what was right in front of her. So I grabbed a sweater, a new book I'd been waiting to start, a cup of coffee, and headed outside. It was absolutely lovely.

Mollie helped me realize that I have been robbing myself of today's happiness by constantly dreaming of the future and ignoring the present. I have been postponing happiness to a later date that never seems to arrive. By tying my happiness to this future version of life, I have kept myself from fully enjoying the goodness God has already placed around me.

Since that realization I have learned to practice what I call *Godly Mindfulness*, which means I try to spend time appreciating the present moment and all that God is doing around me. Maybe that means watching my boys play football in the backyard or enjoying the hummingbirds at the feeder. It's drinking in all the ways God is at work both in the big and the small.

Paul knew this was true when he said, "Godliness with contentment is great gain" (1 Timothy 6:6). When we're content with what we've already been given, we have all we could ever want. More than looking toward what the future might hold, look to enjoy what God's given you now.

Take five minutes to think about all the ways God has provided for you and the ways He brings you happiness. Record those things here or in your journal.

_____

_____

_____

_____

I'LL BE HAPPY WHEN . . .

We all have the tendency to say, "I'll be happy when . . ." For some it is, "I'll be happy when I get married," or "I'll be happy when we have kids," or "I'll be happy when the kids are out of diapers," or "I'll be happy when all the kids are in school."

Every one of us has the thought that when _____ happens, we'll finally be happy. But all this mentality does is rob us of the happiness we can experience today. Instead of enjoying the happiness God offers us now, we put our happiness off to a future date that never seems to roll around.

It's as if we're waiting for our future life to give us what God has already given us for today.

God designed us to find our contentment and happiness in Him no matter what our circumstances are. Think about what Paul says in Philippians 4:12: "I know what it is to be in need, and I know what it is to have plenty. I have learned the secret of being content in any and every situation, whether well fed or hungry, whether living in plenty or in want."

Do you know why Paul was able to be content in every circumstance?

Because Paul was able to do all things through Christ who gave him strength (Philippians 4:13).

At every turn in Paul's life, whether for good or bad, Paul found his happiness in Jesus.

In Jesus we can choose to be happy now. That's great news for *today*!

Can you think of some ways you have put off happiness? Maybe you've put your happiness off until you're in a different season of life or have achieved a certain goal. Journal what you're putting your happiness on hold for and then list out three reasons you can be happy right now.

_____

_____

_____

_____

_____

A PICTURE IS WORTH A THOUSAND GOOD FEELINGS

I love to take pictures every day with my phone. Taking pictures of the boys doing something silly, a beautiful sunset, my friends smiling—I love capturing these moments. I once took more than 250 photos in one day just because I love documenting these happy times. Sometimes when I'm in a bad mood, I open my phone and scroll through photos and, like magic, I'm in a great mood!

Of course, not all moments in life are frame-worthy. There are painful memories our minds hold like snapshots in a camera that can be triggered by the smallest thing. When I'm reminded of the less-than-desirable moments in my life, I can get caught up dwelling on them, and it can take me a while to see the good that overwhelmingly outweighs the bad.

It's important to know our triggers and to learn how to combat those negative, happiness-stealing thoughts. For me, opening my phone and scrolling through all the evidence of God's incredible grace in my life is the reminder I need. I see reminders of His generosity at the touch of a button. God's Word also reminds us of His intention for us to be happy people: "I know that there is nothing better for people than to be happy and to do good while they live" (Ecclesiastes 3:12).

Your triggers and your resets are unique to you. Maybe your journal is a way you remind yourself of God's goodness. Maybe it's found in spending time with friends or family. Whatever it is, remembering to celebrate happiness in the here and now keeps us focused on God's goodness and faithfulness.

Make it a point this week to be aware of the happy moments in your life and to snap a quick picture that you can keep as a future reminder of God's goodness.

_____

_____

_____

_____

_____

_____

TAKE DELIGHT

When people don't receive the answer to prayer they wanted, it's normal to hear, "I thought God wanted me to be happy. If God wants that, why won't He give me this?" It's a valid point, but typically not in the way that we mean. When we say things like this what we're really asking is, "Does God actually care about my happiness?"

There have been so many times in my life when I was sure a certain thing would bring me real happiness. If my house could just look a certain way, or if I could just lose those last five pounds, or if my kids would just do this, then I'd really be happy.

When I get stuck thinking this way, I'll pray for weeks on end until a funny thing starts to happen. As I'm praying for the thing I'm convinced will make me happy, over time, the thing that I'm praying for starts to change.

Instead of my kids miraculously developing a clean streak to rival Mary's sister Martha, I remind myself of the fact that maybe I was expecting a little too much and "good enough" around the house is sometimes perfect.

Instead of obsessing and praying and demanding those last few pounds melt away, I find myself immensely grateful for health and the strength to fulfill God's calling for my life.

The more time I spend with God, the more time He spends changing me, aligning me more with His desires and less with mine. My happiness becomes less wrapped up in getting this or that and instead becomes wrapped up in Him.

He becomes the desire of my heart. As David says in Psalm 37:4, "Take delight in the LORD, and he will give you the desires of your heart." When our delight is in God, our troubles don't melt away, but our perspective shifts, and He becomes the place our happiness is found.

Today, ask yourself, how can you align your desires with those of God? Spend time and ask God to help you find your delight in Him.

_____

_____

_____

FAITH IT 'TIL YOU MAKE IT

You may have heard the phrase, "Fake it 'til you make it." But instead of that, I say, "Faith it 'til you make it."

The Bible is filled with those whose entire lives could've been lived under the truth of that phrase. Noah waited years until the flood happened. Abraham had to wait decades before God gave him the son he was promised. David had to wait years until he was crowned king, even though he was given the promise when he was a boy.

I'm so thankful that God has given us these examples of what it looks like to live by faith, waiting on His promises to be fulfilled. Every one of the heroes from God's Word expressed his own anxiety, wondering what God was up to and why He was taking so long. Yet they remained faithful until God was ready to move. They didn't have to fake it, and we don't either!

Don't live out of a place of faking it; believe in faith that God is working right now! Mark 11 reminds us, "I tell you, whatever you ask for in prayer, believe that you have received it, and it will be yours" (v. 24). We may not feel as if we've arrived yet or that our lives look like we think they should. Even if we're still waiting on the promises of God to take effect, we can live out of a place of faith that God will redeem every situation for His glory and our good. It's called hope. And people who have hope are happier people.

> What is something you are believing in faith that God will provide in your life? Write about it and thank Him in advance for His provision.
>
> _____
>
> _____
>
> _____
>
> _____
>
> _____
>
> _____
>
> _____

WHAT'S SO GOOD ABOUT TODAY?

As a mother of five boys, you could say my life is slightly busy. From school to sports practices to appointments to church to friends (multiplied by five), it can seem as if our lives go from thing to thing at breakneck speed. But in the moments when life takes a breather, I get a chance to reflect on how fast all of it seems to be passing by.

I'm constantly reminded of how careful I need to be so I don't miss the things God has placed right in front of me now.

When we were kids, it felt as if we couldn't wait to get to the next stage in life, be it first grade, middle school, or getting our driver's license. And for most of us, that feeling of wanting to hurry toward what's next hasn't left.

We still find ourselves looking toward the horizon of our lives, completely unaware of the happiness of the here and now.

I remind myself to be careful not to be in such a rush to get to the next stage, the next achievement, or the next new thing that I miss out on what God wants me to enjoy about today. He wants me to savor the day with a patient endurance. The book of James reminds us,

"Let endurance have its perfect result, so that you may be perfect and complete, lacking in nothing" (1:4 NASB). I must continually look away from what God has next to see what God has now.

In the light of savoring what God has for me now, that fifth grade recorder concert becomes an off-key joy, the first Thanksgiving break with our college freshman back home with us becomes a celebration, and even that middle-of-the-night race to help a middle schooler with his project becomes a fun challenge.

Think about your life right now. Ask yourself, *What is good today?* Write it down, and consider making it a daily practice to write a simple sentence that says, "Today, [fill in the blank] is good."

_____

_____

_____

_____

LOOKING FOR PERFECTION

We were running late to church one Sunday morning. One kid couldn't find the shoes he wanted to wear, another had spilled his breakfast on the floor, and one son was still asleep in bed. Mark was trying his best to corral the other two, while I was hurriedly trying to finish putting on my makeup and simultaneously eating Cheerios out of a coffee mug.

I have this imaginary picture of what a Sunday morning could look like, where we all sit down for a beautiful breakfast spread, get ready without any fuss, then take a leisurely and pleasant ride to church. Rarely does my life look like the perfect scenes I imagine for myself or my family, and in those moments when life doesn't look as I hoped it would, I'm tempted to let my circumstances steal my joy.

If we're honest, all of us have believed the lie that our situation needs to be perfect for us to be happy. We might never say that our expectation is perfection, but when our life looks less than perfect, our disappointment says it all.

Even though we know in our heads that perfection will never be gained this side of heaven, we forget to live that way in our daily lives. First Corinthians 13:10 tells us, "When the perfect comes, the partial will be done away" (NASB).

Our God knew we would never reach perfection on our own, which is why He sent Jesus! Jesus is the only source of perfection we will know in this life. When life looks imperfect, look to the perfect Savior.

Today, celebrate happiness in the here and now by celebrating what is imperfectly wonderful in your life. Describe one thing in your life that is imperfectly wonderful.

_____

_____

_____

_____

_____

_____

PROGRESS, NOT PERFECTION

One of the greatest joys of raising our kids has been watching them learn and grow, especially in the early years. There's a sense of wonder and joy that we share with our kids as we watch them go from sitting to crawling, from crawling to standing, and from standing to walking. At that stage in their life, it doesn't matter how many steps they take or even how many times they fall down. We're just thrilled that they're taking steps!

As my kids have grown, it's slowly dawned on me that God looks at us the same way. He celebrates our steps and delights when we move closer toward Him. I used to think that God had a tally sheet in heaven, marking every stumble against every step, and if I had enough steps He'd really be happy with me. But God isn't looking for perfection; He's celebrating our progress!

The truth is, we are all on a journey, and we won't arrive at our destination in this lifetime. Until then, our heavenly Father stands with His arms open, ready to receive us as we take our next steps toward Him. The book of Isaiah says, "Whether you turn to the right or to the left, your ears will hear a voice behind you, saying, 'This is the way; walk in it'" (30:21). Our God has already taken the steps to provide us with His perfection in Jesus. All He asks is for us to walk forward as He celebrates the progress we've made along the way.

> Where are you tempted to strive for perfection instead of celebrating progress? Today, rest in the truth that your God delights in every step forward.

_____

_____

_____

_____

_____

_____

_____

REFLECTION

_____

_____

_____

_____

_____

_____

_____

_____

_____

_____

_____

_____

4

GOOD FRIENDS AND HAPPY HEARTS

You were created for community.

LEAN ON ME

Have you ever met someone you instantly knew you wanted to learn something from? Maybe it was the way she spoke or how she presented herself, but you just immediately knew, *I have to get to know this person.*

I've had the pleasure of knowing a few women like this in my life. They are fiercely faithful women of God who have been an example to me of what a truly happy life can look like. From these women I've learned so much about what it means to be a loving and honoring wife, a nurturing and fun mom, and a closer follower of Jesus. I am blessed to call them my mentors and my friends.

We all need these kinds of women in our lives, women whose footsteps we can follow. These are women whose life examples have said, like Paul, "Follow my example, as I follow the example of Christ" (1 Corinthians 11:1). When you're in a new season of life and need godly women to learn from and lean on, wait for God to show you who you can begin to intentionally invite into your life.

Ask the Lord to provide two or three people who will encourage you in your faith and spiritual maturity throughout your year of happy—people who have earned your trust and whose own lives bear good fruit. Often we find those women through groups in our local churches. Write their names as the Lord provides. As God directs you, talk with them about fulfilling this role in your life (and maybe even tell them why you felt God chose them for you).

_____

_____

_____

_____

_____

YOUR FAVORITE FIVE

I heard a wise man say, "You're the average of the five people you spend the most time with."[1] For many of us, we spend the majority of our time with our immediate families (which explains why I could only speak in two syllable words when all five of my boys were little)! But seriously, this quote challenged me to think about the friends I spend the majority of my time with. Are they positive and encouraging or negative and critical?

When we begin to spend most of our time around negative and critical people, it's pretty easy to see what happens. Instead of being quick to encourage others, we're quick to critique. Instead of seeing the positive in situations, we're quick to complain. We end up getting caught in the same negativity they're stuck in. God's Word warns us, "Do not be misled: 'Bad company corrupts good character'" (1 Corinthians 15:33).

But when we find ourselves surrounded by positive and encouraging people, the opposite is true. We're moved to be generous with our words and quick to affirm. We feel recharged and refreshed because of how life-giving they are. We're encouraged by their example to be the best versions of ourselves.

Pray that God will help you see who in your life is building you up and who is a negative influence on your life. Decide to spend more of your time with your friends who make your life better! List the five people in your life who encourage, support, and love you the most. As you decide whom to invest most of your time with, focus on these fab five.

_____

_____

_____

_____

_____

_____

_____

FIND YOUR BATTLE BUDDIES

A friend of mine shared with me that in the army they have something called *battle buddies*. A battle buddy is someone who supports you and looks out for you in and out of combat. They're always there to keep an eye out for your emotional and physical health, whether you're in the trenches or the barracks. I love this concept.

Isn't it true that we all need just a couple of great battle buddies on this journey with us? We all need friends who encourage us, look out for us, and are there to battle with us on the good days and the hard days.

Solomon says it like this in the book of Proverbs, "As iron sharpens iron, so one person sharpens another" (27:17). Just as a blacksmith will use metal on metal to form it for its intended purpose, God will use certain people in our lives to sharpen and mold us into who He's making us to be. These people are the ones God places in our foxholes.

They'll call out areas of potential danger in our lives and encourage us to be who we were created to be. They'll lovingly and faithfully walk with us, even when our lives look more like a battlefield than we might want to admit.

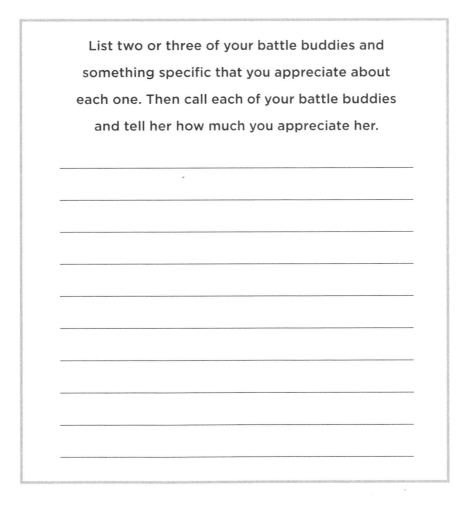

List two or three of your battle buddies and
something specific that you appreciate about
each one. Then call each of your battle buddies
and tell her how much you appreciate her.

_____

_____

_____

_____

_____

_____

_____

_____

_____

ASSUME THE BEST

When Mark and I were dating, going to the movies was our thing. Technically it was my thing. I love going to the movies. There's no experience like it, and I don't care what anyone says, no home theater can match the magic of going to the actual movies. Soon after we were married, Mark informed me that he preferred the couch and TV to stadium seats and the big screen. What a bait and switch. Or at least that's the way I took it!

After months of missing out on some really great movies, I melted down. I whined, and pouted, and stomped my feet, declaring he would *not* be taking my precious theater-going ways from me. He laughed and said, "Alli, I didn't say you can't go to the movies. I just want you to go with someone who will enjoy it as much as you do!"

Boy, did I get that all wrong. I assumed the worst of Mark, when really, he was only thinking of my happiness.

One key to being happier in life is to assume the best in people, that they are operating to the best of their ability, and they mean you no harm. When you decide to err on the side of assuming others have good motives, you protect yourself from living with a negative mind-set.

Even more than that, when we decide to assume the best about people, we're deciding to love them. We're choosing to trust that they're not out to get us, or trying to take something from us. First Corinthians explains how love "always protects, always trusts, always hopes, always perseveres" (13:7). And, best of all, we're actually protecting the relationship and each other's happiness, letting love guide our assumptions about each other's motives instead of preparing for disappointment or hurt.

It may seem weird, but Mark and I have a stronger, happier marriage now that he doesn't go to the movies with me. Instead, I go to new movies with my girlfriends or my sons, and Mark and I snuggle up and watch them at home. That makes us both happy! It's a win-win!

Think about a situation where you didn't assume the best about someone and they turned out to be completely innocent. What can you learn from that situation?

_____

_____

_____

THE $133,000 RAISE?

Researchers have determined that spending time with friends you like increases your happiness as much as if you had a $133,000 per year raise.[1] Of course, we know money does not buy happiness, but it's fascinating to think that scientists compared people who made tons of money every year with those who lived in great communities, and they found the happiness levels to be the same.

It's tempting to think how much happier we'd be if we had all those extra funds, but once again, scientists are only affirming what God has already said. Still, I wonder, how many of us consider our time with our friends as valuable as a six-figure raise?

I bet Solomon did! Solomon knew the value of true friendship and said in Ecclesiastes 4:9–10, "Two are better than one, because they have a good return for their labor: if either of them falls down, one can help the other up."

God has given us friends to keep us rooted in His purpose in our lives. When we begin to lose sight of the work God's doing in our lives, our friends and community are there to help us get back on track and refocus on Him.

In friendship, we see Jesus' love on display as we lay our lives down to help each other back up.

Though a six-figure raise probably isn't available to most of us, friends and community are. List the names of three to five people who make you feel happy after you spend time with them. Make plans today to get together again soon!

_____

_____

_____

_____

_____

_____

_____

_____

INVESTING IN OTHERS

The happiest seasons in my life have come when I've made the choice to intentionally invest my time in others. When I've set aside a morning, a lunch meeting, or an evening, and made space in my world for the express purpose of pouring into others, I feel happier.

There is so much joy that comes from knowing you've made a difference in the life of someone else just by being available and willing.

One of my coaching clients does this so well. She intentionally pours into others (even though she is an incredibly busy mama, entrepreneur, and wife). Each week she does three intentional things to help others. Every Sunday she serves on the parking team at her church and makes it a point to help young moms get all their kiddos out of the car and into the church building. Then on Monday, she writes an encouragement card to a young mom she saw at church on Sunday. And then sometime during the week, she intentionally prays for a friend and texts that person to let them know she has prayed.

It's amazing how much happiness that brings her, and, having been on the receiving end of her thoughtfulness, I know how much happiness it brings others. Hebrews tells us, "God is not unjust; he will not forget your work and the love you have shown him as you have helped his people and continue to help them" (6:10).

Our happiness in life doesn't come from the things we acquire, but from the people we inspire. When we take the time to invest in others through our resources, time, finances, or words of encouragement, it builds our happiness and joy. God has freely invested in our lives so that we would freely invest in the lives of others.

What are some simple ways you can begin to invest in the lives of others? Ask God to give you the name of someone who needs your encouragement today. Then act!

_____

_____

_____

_____

_____

LOOK AT THE FRUIT

My friend Emily is one of the happiest people I know. She oozes joy, and, honestly, I don't know how she does it. She's a single mom, works two jobs, and has a daughter with severe special needs that make her medically fragile. So how in the world Emily has time to even think about anyone else is beyond me. But she does!

If I get a new haircut, she makes me feel as if it's the best thing she's ever seen. If I get a bad review on a book, she makes me believe that it must be a fluke, because in her eyes I'm the best author on the face of the planet. Emily radiates happiness, and she makes me want to do that for others.

Something happens when we spend time around life-giving people; we start to become life-giving people ourselves. It seems so obvious, but I've forgotten on more than one occasion that the people I spend my time with help determine the person I'm becoming.

The times when I've been the most generous, contented, joy-filled, happy, and loving have been when I've sought out and spent time with people who exemplify all those qualities.

Remember, if you want to know who you'll be in the future, just look at the five people you spend the most time with. Matthew tells us, "By their fruit you will recognize them" (7:20). Their fruit might someday become the fruit of your life as well.

The fruit of our lives is determined by the roots of our relationships.

Take time to write down the fruit you want to see in your own heart and life. Ask God to show you others in your life who can help you grow this fruit by their own examples.

_____

_____

_____

_____

_____

_____

CHECKING YOUR SURROUNDINGS

We all know toxic people in the worlds we occupy. These people can't help but point out the negative in everything that surrounds them. They act out of their hurts and deep wounds, trying to level the playing field of life so that others can know their pain. Instead of building others up, they seek to bring us down to where they are.

You know them. I know them. Sometimes we are them.

It is tempting to think that maybe we will be able to pull our friend out of that pit. We think that maybe if we show them enough positivity and life, we can affect life-giving change that invites them out of a seemingly endless cycle of self-destruction. The problem is, more often than not, we end up like a lifeguard with no floatation device, getting pulled down by the person we are trying to rescue.

God's Word often talks about how important the people we surround ourselves with are. In Proverbs 14:7, it says, "Stay away from a fool, for you will not find knowledge on their lips." The fool is someone who won't listen to sound advice or encouragement, but will continue in her own way despite the warnings of others. While God calls us to encourage others in love, the fool has totally rejected God's Word and can't even accept it.

We can't live the abundant life God planned for us if we are surrounded by fools and the consequences of their bad choices.

Instead, we can choose to surround ourselves with those who desire to grow and desire to help us grow also. When we surround ourselves with those who seek after life, we will be able to help others do the same.

Who are the friends God has placed in your life to help build you up? Thank Him for them, and ask Him to surround you with others who will help you do the same.

_____

_____

_____

_____

_____

_____

DIVING INTO THE DEEP END OF RELATIONSHIPS

As a kid, I was always slightly intimidated by the deep end of the pool. You could say the deep end and I had something of a strained relationship. I loved it because the diving board was there, but I also felt a little nervous because I could never quite make out where the bottom was.

The deep end offered adventure, but the shallow end was safe and predictable.

Eventually, what was true in the pool became true in my relationships with others. In the shallow end of relationships, I didn't have to worry because I wasn't vulnerable to getting in over my head.

In the shallow end, I could make sure that my mascara never slid down my cheeks and that my hair mostly stayed put.

In the shallow end, where I can keep up appearances, I always look good.

But we were never meant to live life in the shallow end. We were made to know the depths of joy that come when we dive into the deep end of relationships. It's in the deep end of life where adventure happens. Sure, our feet aren't always on solid ground, but it's there where we find community because we are loved for who we are by people who know us as we are.

In the deep end, there's no need to try to be perfect because deep friendships find joy in being gloriously imperfect.

From the very beginning, God said it wasn't good for man to be alone, and that's still true today. Ecclesiastes says this about relationships: "If either of them falls down, one can help the other up. But pity anyone who falls and has no one to help them up" (4:10). When we're known, we're able to be loved, and when we're loved, we're able to know joy.

Today, make the decision to dive into the deep end of your relationships. Think about the people in your life who know the "real" you. Write them a note and thank them for allowing you to be yourself with them.

_____

_____

_____

_____

_____

REFLECTION

_____

_____

_____

_____

_____

_____

_____

_____

_____

_____

_____

_____

5

FINDING YOUR HAPPY THOUGHT

Where your thoughts go, your happiness follows.

THE DISCIPLINE
OF GRATITUDE

"Mom, today I'm happy about the Steelers winning the big game, double-stuffed Oreos, and snow."

Since my boys were tiny, I've asked them every night to share three things they are grateful for from the day. Sometimes they share their wins, sometimes they share silly things, and occasionally they open up with great depths of gratitude for something during the day.

This practice established a discipline of gratitude for my family, which is a building block to real happiness. I've seen it in my boys as they've grown up, finding things to be grateful for, and finding the happiness that comes with gratitude along the way.

Multiple studies show that when people keep track of things to be grateful for, not only do they feel better, but that gratitude reaches other areas of their life as well.[1] Researchers are finding that what God teaches us in the Bible is true, proving that gratitude is the key to happiness and overcoming anxiety. God created us to live gratitude-filled lives. We are to be grateful to Him and grateful to see Him at work, giving thanks in all things.

Paul says this in 1 Thessalonians 5:16–18: "Rejoice always, pray continually, give thanks in all circumstances; for this is God's will for you in Christ Jesus."

God has made us to live in a constant state of gratitude toward Him in everything He provides. And when we live with that design in mind, we can know the happiness that's waiting for us there.

Think of three things you can be thankful for. Identifying three things that you are grateful for every day sounds so simple, but don't let the simplicity fool you. The daily practice of the discipline of gratitude will make you happier, reduce your anxiety, and help keep you focused on all the good God is doing in your life.

_____

_____

_____

_____

RENEWING YOUR MIND

Growing up in the South, I often heard the phrase, "Cleanliness is next to godliness." To a little kid, it sounded like something from the Bible. Because I thought it was from God's Word, I let it carry a lot of weight in my life growing up, so imagine my surprise when I learned it wasn't even in the Bible!

I was pretty shocked when I learned the truth about the phrase, but I was also relieved. You know why? Because my holiness was no longer measured by the cleanliness of my room. I was freed from a law that God never gave.

The world's truth can often seem like God's truth, and sometimes it's hard to tell the difference.

So how can we know what truth is from God and what truth is from the world? God's truth will always line up with His Word and leads us closer to Him.

In Romans 12:2, Paul says, "Do not conform to the pattern of this world, but be transformed by the renewing of your mind. Then you will be able to test and approve what God's will is—his good, pleasing and perfect will."

When we begin to trade the world's wisdom for God's truth, we'll experience the happiness of being in His will.

What ways have you been "conform[ed] to the pattern of this world" in the ways you think? Record all that you can think of. Ask God to renew your mind according to His Word so that you can better follow His will.

_____

_____

_____

_____

_____

_____

_____

GRATITUDE IS THE KEY INGREDIENT OF HAPPINESS

"Don't care how, I want it now!"

Who can forget this line sung by the most ungrateful child ever, Veruca Salt, from *Willy Wonka & the Chocolate Factory*. Veruca Salt had it all, and what she didn't have, she often demanded her father give to her immediately. And as we all know from the movie, her father always gave her what she wanted.

But even though Veruca had it all, she was miserably unhappy. She never stopped to appreciate what she had because she was always focused on what she didn't have, or worse yet, what someone else had that she wanted.

Learning to be grateful is taught, and it's a big reason why I practice the "three things you're grateful for" routine with my boys at bedtime.

Identifying three things that we're grateful for at the end of every day is a simple way to reduce anxiety, increase happiness, and set the tone for a great day tomorrow.

Our daily moments of gratitude remind us that, ultimately, we're not in control of our lives. And when our lives lack gratitude, we can slip into a habit of assuming we're owed all the things in life, instead of being filled with gratitude for what God provides.

Our gratitude is the key ingredient to our happiness.

When Jesus teaches His disciples how to pray in Luke 11, he tells them that God is like a father who loves giving good gifts to His kids (vv. 11–13). What a sweet picture of our loving Father. I want to receive His gifts with gratefulness and joy and to teach my children to do the same.

List three things that you are grateful for today. Be sure to download the weekly gratitude printable at AlliWorthington.com/YearofHappy.

_____

_____

_____

_____

_____

_____

DON'T FEED THE FEARS

Have you ever been to a national park where the signs say, "DON'T FEED THE BEARS?" This seems like a no-brainer to me, and I always want to ask, "What fool is feeding the bears?" But apparently some people (a lot of people) need the reminder.

There's a very good reason park rangers don't want us to feed the bears. When bears think that food is available to them (as in when people feed them or leave food out for them), they will essentially take up residence in the heavily populated areas of the park. You can see the problem, right?

Isn't it true that our fears operate in the same way? When we consistently feed them, they take up residence in our hearts and minds, and the longer they are there, the more of a danger to us they become. I think the key to overcoming this is to understand how we are feeding our fears. For example, a couple of years ago, I stopped watching the news every day. I realized that a constant steady stream of bad news was stealing my happiness and giving me anxiety.

My anxiety grew daily thinking about all the terrible things that were happening in the world, which somehow translated to what terrible things could possibly happen to my children. I stayed scared because I was constantly feeding my fears.

Of course, I haven't just stuck my head in the sand, pretending the troubles of the world don't exist. Instead, I've found ways to limit my intake. It's not blissful ignorance that makes me happy. It's taking charge of what I know feeds my fears.

When we feed our fears, we're inviting them to hang around—and it doesn't take long (just like those bears) for them to make themselves right at home. Fears create anxiety and tempt us to think we're in control of our lives. Next time fear comes looking for a meal consider what Peter says in 1 Peter 5:7: "Cast all your anxiety on him because he cares for you." We have a choice here. Instead of feeding the fears, let's feed our trust in God by casting our fears on Him and resting in His care.

What are some things that cause you to feed your fears? Ask God to help you find ways to feed your trust in Him instead of feeding those fears.

_____

_____

_____

OUR THOUGHTS ARE POWERFUL

When my husband was in an especially hard time with an illness, I often found myself thinking, *This is never going to get any better.* I accidentally became my own false prophet of the future and, in the process, stole my own happiness through my negative thought patterns.

I had to learn to replace my negative thoughts with God's truth. Instead of negativity, I learned to say, "God, this is terrible, but I trust You are in control and You will provide everything we need to walk through this. I trust You."

When Paul was going through one of his most trying moments, he reminded the Philippians (and himself) of this in Philippians 4:8, saying, "Whatever is true, whatever is noble, whatever is right, whatever is pure, whatever is lovely, whatever is admirable—if anything is excellent or praiseworthy—think about such things." Our perspective shapes our perception.

We all have hard things that happen in life, but it is our thoughts about those bad things that determine how they affect us. When we fill our minds with thoughts that lead us to trust God, we will be ready when difficult moments come.

Whatever it is that you are going through right now, you can trust Him.

Ask God to help you learn how to stop negative thoughts and replace them with truth. Take one negative thought you have been consistently having and replace it with a truth from God.

_____

_____

_____

_____

_____

_____

_____

WHAT VOICES ARE YOU LISTENING TO?

Growing up, I often heard the phrase, "Garbage in, garbage out." Remember that one? Now that I'm the mother of five boys, you'd better believe they're hearing it too. It's a simple principle, and it stands to reason that what we put in our hearts and minds is what will come out.

In our world, there are voices that constantly fight for our attention and affection. Every show we watch, every post on Facebook, every book we read, every advertisement we run across—everything is trying to get the attention of our ears and imagination. And these voices aren't quiet either—they demand to be heard!

So how do we choose which voices to listen to?

If we're listening to voices that don't lead us to find our happiness in Jesus, it shouldn't surprise us when our lives are lacking in joy. But if we are choosing to listen to voices that point us to the Source of all happiness, our lives will be filled with the fruit of those voices.

We must choose to listen to the ones that give and protect our happiness, because our lives end up looking like the voices we choose to follow. I have to be careful who I'm listening to so I can protect my heart and my happiness.

More than any other voice, let's seek to listen to the voice of God who desires that our joy would be complete. He tells us, "My sheep listen to my voice; I know them, and they follow me" (John 10:27). Listen to His voice, and you will always find the pathway to happiness.

What voices get your attention? Is it the voices of friends, social media, Scripture, devotional guides, or preachers? Make a list of all the things you regularly read, listen to, or give your attention to, and then write an "H" next to the sources that lead you to feel happy. Are there any sources on your list that you want to change? Why or why not?

_____

_____

_____

_____

HOW TO RELEASE OUR WORRIES

If ever there was a mom who understood how it felt to let her child go and to trust God, it was Jochebed, the mother of Moses. I cannot even picture the terror she must have endured when Pharaoh ordered the death of all the Israelite babies. She must have played out a million different ways to save her son from the Egyptians.

So she put him in a waterproof basket and waited for an opportune moment to send him out into the Nile River, hopefully to his safety and not to his death. Can you imagine the death grip she had on that basket? Miraculously, she did what so many of us find impossible to do: she released her baby and his future into the hands of God.

Surrender is no easy feat (even when it doesn't involve floating your baby down a teeming river). It is so easy to hold onto the things that are dear to us—our homes, our jobs, our marriages, our kids. Those are good things, and of course we should hold onto them, as long as we do so in obedience to what God wants for us.

But fear tells us to keep a white-knuckled grip on the things that matter most to us. It leads us to believe that we are constantly on the verge of losing everything. Believing fear keeps us from enjoying life. We are so busy trying to control everything we have just for a moment of peace! But there's no peace in that kind of life.

How do we go from being a stressed-out sister to a faith-filled follower? We must practice the presence of God every day. Read His Word, pray for His peace, and believe His promises for "there is no fear in love . . . perfect love drives out fear" (1 John 4:18). By practicing His presence, we are placing our trust not in what *our* hands can provide but what *His* hands have provided. We are stepping out and acknowledging that we can't accomplish with our worry what God can accomplish with His peace.

Release your worries and receive His peace and power. Sounds like a great trade!

Write out a list of your worries and, one by one, release them to God.

_____

_____

_____

LOVE ONE ANOTHER

When Mark and I were first married, I used to cause all kinds of drama with my need for him to know what I was thinking, feeling, or needing at all times. If he couldn't read my mind, then I'd immediately jump from, "He didn't notice I needed the trash taken out" to "Mark doesn't care about my needs."

I was delightful, right? We laugh about it now, but it was a real challenge in the beginning. I think it's easy for us to believe that just because someone doesn't know what we are thinking or feeling, they must not care for us. But that's simply not true. On any given day, Mark can have a million things going on, from after-school activities, to appliance breakdowns, to the dog needing to go to the vet. Over time, I discovered it is quite possible for Mark to both love me *and* not know what I am thinking or feeling!

The truth is, the Enemy of this world wants to hurt relationships by causing misunderstandings and miscommunication. He does this to steal our happiness. This is why the book of 1 Peter tells us to "be like-minded, be sympathetic, love one another, be compassionate and humble" (3:8). If I become convinced that Mark doesn't know me or doesn't love me (even over simple things like taking out the trash), the Enemy can use those feelings to drive a wedge between us.

Instead, I have learned to give Mark the benefit of the doubt. I believe the best about him instead of believing the worst. It's amazing what a difference this small change in mind-set has made in our marriage.

The next time you want to believe the worst about a person or a situation, try replacing those thoughts by giving that person the benefit of the doubt. Assume the best about him or her and your positive feelings will result in positive actions.

As you think about a troubling person or situation you are currently dealing with, how can you change your thoughts to give that person the benefit of the doubt? Does giving the benefit of the doubt change how you feel about that person or the situation? In what way?

_____

_____

REFLECTION

_____

_____

_____

_____

_____

_____

_____

_____

_____

_____

_____

_____

6

HAPPY IN A WORLD OF CRAZY

You can say no to unnecessary crazy.

LIFE IS NOT A PINTEREST BOARD

I'm not crafty and I don't work out (real talk), so when Pinterest first came out, I really didn't understand why it was so popular. But as its popularity grew, it kind of became my go-to place for inspiration. Want to go on a dream vacation, throw a picture-perfect birthday party, or dazzle people with my culinary skills? With Pinterest, I was just one click away from envy-inducing perfection.

Over time, I developed a love-hate relationship with Pinterest. Sure, I loved collecting thousands of images of places I dream of visiting and fancy complicated recipes I'll never cook. But all of that perfection conflicted with one fundamental part of me: I'm not a perfectionist.

Instead of feeling inspired by the ideas, I felt guilty that I wasn't living up to some unrealistic expectation. I finally had to ask myself, *Who am I trying to impress with all this?*

That's what happens when we subconsciously compare our real life to the perfectly planned, propped, and prepared images on Pinterest: it steals our happiness. The book of Galatians instructs us, "Each one should test their own actions. Then they can take pride in themselves alone, without comparing themselves to someone else, for each one should carry their own load" (6:4–5).

When we are living the lives we were created to live in the way we were created to live them, we find happiness and contentment. So don't let Pinterest (or perfection) steal your happiness this year. Be content with the person God has created you to be and the simple way He calls us to enjoy our lives. For me, that's having small family birthday parties with all my guys sitting around our family table. None of us really enjoys big, elaborate (exhausting) parties, so embracing how God made us and having small, family-only parties actually makes us happier as a family. (And it's budget-friendly too! Bonus!)

As an extra challenge to yourself, for the next seven days take a break from something you do that often leaves you feeling "less than." Journal your thoughts during those seven days and see if you don't discover some freedom!

_____

_____

THE STOP-DOING LIST

Within the first five minutes of just about every day, I'm already reminding myself of all the things I need to do. When I walk into the kitchen, I'm reminded of more things I need to do. And when I see my Bible on the coffee table, I'm reminded of even more things I need to do. Before long, my twenty-four-hour day is packed with thirty hours of things to do.

When my daily schedule gets overrun with too many to-dos, there's typically a reason why. I'd like to say it's because I'm Superwoman and can knock them out with my super strength and speed. Yet, it's far more likely that my motivation for my overpacked schedule is that I'll feel guilty if I take something off it.

If I want to be a good wife, mom, business owner, and writer of course I have to do all these things. And if I'm not doing all the things on my list, then I'm not being faithful to what God's given me, right?

Wrong.

I'm reminded of the time Jesus goes to Mary and Martha's house. While Martha works tirelessly to cook and clean for her guests, Mary chooses to sit at Jesus' feet. And when Martha complains to Jesus that Mary isn't helping, Jesus says, "You are worried and upset about many things, but few things are needed—or indeed only one. Mary has chosen what is better, and it will not be taken away from her" (Luke 10:41–42). Mary did the only thing necessary—she sat at Jesus' feet.

Just imagine how different our lives might look if we stopped moving, stopped piling more work on ourselves, and simply spent some time sitting at the feet of Jesus.

> Instead of piling on more work, spend some time with the Lord and ask Him to reveal to you what things you need to let go of in order to live a happier life in Him. Ask Him to clear out the things that are not His will. As He guides you, write out three things that are going on your stop-doing list.
>
> _____
>
> _____
>
> _____

FROM OUT OF CONTROL TO GRACE

From time to time, I struggle with PTTD. What's PTTD? Post-traumatic toddler disorder. If you've made it to the other side of the terrible twos and tyrannical threes, you know what I'm talking about. All of my boys are well past these years, but every now and again I'll be hit with a flashback of those precious moments, and my eyelids fidget. Tantrums in Target. Wailing in Walmart. Biting the babysitter(s). Refusing to move because we wouldn't let them swim outside in January.

Though we're tempted to think that those moments are limited to our toddlers, let's not kid ourselves. These moments happen to us too.

Just like our toddlers, when our overloaded schedules and the demands of our lives become too much for us to deal with, we become overwhelmed with out-of-control emotions.

When we are more anxious or more irritable than normal, it's a good time to go to Jesus and ask what activities or responsibilities aren't meant for us. Which activities bear more fruit than others? Galatians tells us, "The fruit of the Spirit is love, joy, peace, forbearance, kindness, goodness, faithfulness, gentleness and self-control. Against such things there is no law. Those who belong to Christ Jesus have crucified the flesh with its passions and desires" (5:22–24).

Sometimes we have to say no, even to good things, if we are to stay emotionally healthy.

Ask Jesus which activities and responsibilities are placing too many demands on your life and are causing your emotions to become out-of-control. Then release the things He leads you to release. Journal your thoughts and any insights He gives you.

_____

_____

_____

_____

_____

_____

SEASONS AND CAPACITY LEVELS

There are times when I miss the baby phase of raising kids. The coos and cuddles, the giggles and gassy smiles. So much of it was absolutely wonderful. But, then again, if you asked me if I'd have another kid, I would tell you that you're crazy. This womb is closed for business.

There's a level of freedom I enjoy now that I didn't have when the little guys were around. I was so busy all the time changing diapers, feeding, burping, pumping, and putting them down for naps that I had very few moments to myself.

I'm often amazed at the capacity I had to get things done when I was raising our babies. I mean, imagine applying for a job that had the same hours (and sleep schedule) as it takes to raise an infant. My life now seems like a cakewalk compared to those days.

Thankfully, no season in life lasts forever. We have the crazy-busy seasons (like the infant years), we have the calm seasons (like the empty-nest years), and we have all the seasons in between. The book of Ecclesiastes tells us, "There is a time for everything, and a season for every activity under the heavens" (3:1).

Our capacity for how much we take on is dependent on the season we are in. But when we are in a season where we have very limited capacity for anything extra, it can seem as if we will we be stuck there forever. The good news is seasons change, and before you know it, you might even look back on those crazy-busy times with fondness.

Identify how much capacity you have in this season. Draw a battery (like the one on your phone) and color in how much battery life you feel you have left. If you're feeling as if you don't have enough capacity for the season you're in, reduce your to-do list so you can manage your must-dos. You'll be happier for it!

_____

_____

_____

_____

_____

ON CLARITY AND CLOSED DOORS

In a world filled with open doors of opportunities and obligations, how in the world are we supposed to know which doors to walk through?

Which ones are opportunities sent by God and which ones are obligations we have convinced ourselves we should do?

You know what I do when I can't decide what to do?

I pray for God to close doors. He won't close the ones that are from Him.

It makes sense to me that the Enemy of the world wants to confuse me with open doors that are not from God. Conversely then it also makes sense to me that if I pray for God to close doors, He's not going to close the ones that are from Him! I love how the apostle James wrote it: "If any of you lacks wisdom, you should ask God, who gives generously to all without finding fault, and it will be given to you" (1:5).

When I feel confused by too many open doors, I remember this: God does not obligate me to anything. He has given me free will and the opportunity to choose Him, love Him, and serve Him.

Opportunity is much different than obligation. Lives filled with obligation are not happy lives. They take on a grim and often dark view of the world. But lives filled with opportunities are brighter, more positive, and yes . . . happier.

Take a few minutes to ask God about a decision you are struggling with in your life. Pray and ask God to close doors. The one that is left open will be from Him.

_____

_____

_____

_____

_____

_____

_____

_____

THE ATTITUDE
FOR HAPPINESS

I was once asked to lead a committee, and I said yes before I ever asked myself (or the Lord) if I should do it, if I had the time to do it, or if I had the necessary skills and resources to do it.

If I had stopped to ask those three questions, I might have saved myself (and others) a whole lot of frustration. Instead, I just plowed through, hating every moment of the experience, and making everyone else involved hate it (or me) too!

Turns out, my attitude about the work to be done had a great influence on the work itself, on the people I was leading, and on how I would feel about myself when the task was complete.

In that season of my life, I said yes a lot. And consequently, I was miserable. I thought that if I could just grit my teeth and gut it out, I would be able to get through anything. Let me tell you, I was a real peach to be around back in those days!

Our attitude has everything to do with how we go about doing the things asked of us. (And all the parents in the back said, "Amen!") Our attitude toward something defines how we think about it, which in turn determines how we'll act, and at the end of the day, how we will feel about ourselves.

That is especially true of our response to the things God has called us to do. His Word tells us, "Whether you eat or drink or whatever you do, do it all for the glory of God" (1 Corinthians 10:31). All too often it's easy to drudge through life, living out our calling with a heart of obligation instead of a heart of joy.

God created us to be happy, to find joy in the things He has called us to do in this world. And that's something I can say "YES" to!

Today, ask yourself what you have been doing with a negative attitude, and write down some thoughts on how you can change that. You'll be happier with the outcome and with yourself when your attitude reflects a positive change.

_____

_____

_____

GET MOVING

When I start to feel stressed and sluggish, a few common threads begin to weave themselves into my life. One of them is that I stop exercising. To me, it seems like exercise is the one thing in my schedule that I don't *really* have to do. In fact, if you know me at all, you know that I think putting on yoga pants and just thinking about working out should count as my workout for the day. Most of the time, the idea of exercise feels like icing on the cake of a bad day. (Just keeping it real here.)

But researchers tell us again and again that exercise is both physically and emotionally beneficial to us.[1] Not only are we more physically alert when we are exercising, but we also see noticeable improvements in our overall mental and emotional health. It just feels good!

Living a happy life that's on mission for the kingdom means we need to be strong—physically, spiritually, and emotionally. Even if it's a simple twenty-minute walk, get out and get some endorphins going to feel happier! God's Word asks us, "Do you not know that your bodies are temples of the Holy Spirit, who is in you, whom you have received from God? You are not your own; you were bought at a price. Therefore honor God with your bodies" (1 Corinthians 6:19–20).

And even though I still have a love-hate relationship with working out, I love the way I feel afterward, and I love knowing I'm doing my part to live a happy, healthy life.

What can you start to do today that will help you get moving? Find a friend or two who can start this exercise journey with you to keep you motivated and accountable.

_____

_____

_____

_____

_____

_____

_____

ESCAPING THE TYRANNY OF THE URGENT

We must really amuse God. We run around trying to do so much, constantly searching for a rhythm in a world of being overwhelmed. The reality is that if we were to slow down and ask Him what is actually important, we might be surprised by what He could accomplish through us. Ephesians tells us that God "is able to do immeasurably more than all we ask or imagine, according to his power that is at work within us" (3:20).

The tyranny of the urgent tells us that what's important is what's now. We live our lives as slaves to the incessant needs of this tyrant, always feeling as if we're running behind and never able to catch up. There are too many e-mails left unanswered, there are ten voicemails you haven't responded to, there's way too much laundry you've left on the floor, not to mention the dinner you still haven't made for your family.

When our lives are dominated by the tyranny of the urgent, there's little room left for God or others, much less any time for ourselves. We can't serve two masters. We need to unlearn the habits that keep us perpetually busy and learn how to leave what's undone for tomorrow. It can wait.

We can take a breath, slow down, and take a moment to consider if all our movement is actually helping us accomplish the important things in life.

That text can go unanswered if it takes us away from time with God. That e-mail response can wait if it means you get enough sleep tonight. That task can wait if it means you get to spend quality time with your family.

The urgent is a tyrant king. But fortunately, the King we serve has set us free to live a life that brings us joy.

What habits have you made that keep you a slave to the tyranny of the urgent? Today, take a moment to slow down and ask God to show you what's truly important.

_____

_____

_____

_____

_____

ENOUGH

Sometimes it feels as if our world is constantly telling us to do more and have more. We feel like to be truly satisfied with the way our lives are going we need to check all the boxes the world tells us to. Impossibly healthy lifestyle? Check. Way too expensive vacations? Check. Perfect home decor? (Shiplap, anyone?) Check.

How many of us find ourselves spending insane amounts of effort attempting to complete the world's to-do list only to realize that the list never actually ends? We spend our precious time trying to do more and have more, hoping that we won't miss out on all that life has to offer. (FOMO is real, y'all.) Am I the only one who wants to shout, "Enough!" and tap out of this craziness?

In the moments I'm tempted to believe enough will never be enough, I'm reminded of God's care for the Israelites in the wilderness. Even when they made a terrible mess out of their lives, it didn't change how God provided for them. Every morning there was fresh manna to eat.

When the to-do list of our lives seems to scream that we don't have enough or haven't done enough, our Father gives us our daily bread. Do you feel the freedom that comes with that truth? Our God personally considers our needs and provides for us. Jesus tells us, "Do not worry about your life, what you will eat or drink; or about your body, what you will wear. Is not life more than food, and the body more than clothes? Look at the birds of the air; they do not sow or reap or store away in barns, and yet your heavenly Father feeds them. Are you not much more valuable than they?" (Matthew 6:25–26). We are freed from our worry to be more and have more when we trust His provision.

Friend, where are you tempted to feel as if you need more than what God provides? Write those things below, on the Reflection page at the end of this section, or in your journal. Today, rest in the truth that our God provides all we need for today.

_____

_____

_____

_____

REFLECTION

7

WHEN HAPPINESS IS HARD

When you fight for your joy, it's always worth it.

POURING IN WHAT IS GOOD

I love to feed my backyard hummingbirds during the summer. I make them new food every Sunday afternoon with a solution of water, sugar, and a few drops of red dye. It's amazing how the whole pitcher of water is transformed by a few little drops of red food coloring. With one quick stir, the water turns red.

Isn't that what a painful experience can do to us? The pain from one experience can color our lives just like those few drops of red dye color that water.

The only way to get the red dye out of the water is to keep pouring fresh water in until it runs the red out. When we are hurt, we have to keep pouring in what is good, what is healthy, and what is helpful until the pain is run out too.

On the night before Jesus' death, He left His disciples with the following words: "I have told you these things, so that in me you may have peace. In the world you will have trouble. But take heart! I have overcome the world" (John 16:33). Jesus knows the pain and brokenness of our lives and has given us peace through His pain.

In the painful moments of life, I pour in this truth. Even though we'll know pain in this world, Jesus has overcome that pain. And like an overflow of fresh water, the dye of my pain dissolves as it's overcome by His peace.

As you make the choice for a year of happy, think about a painful experience that you are ready to let go, to grow from, and to move on from. If it helps you, journal about the pain you have felt or are feeling now and write out how you can intentionally pour in God's goodness. Then start pouring in extra portions of what makes you happy, what builds you up, and keep going until the pain has been overcome by the goodness of God. Journal the experience as you go.

_____

_____

_____

THE IMPORTANCE OF SHOWING UP

It was Friday morning, and I was running on empty. After a long week of meetings and after-school taxi driving, I was ready for a little me time. And yet, there was my phone giving me *another* reminder of my nine o'clock meeting with a dear friend who needed my ear. Ugh. I gave myself a little pep talk (one I often use when I don't want to do something). I said, "Alli, put your big girl pants on, get in the car, and just show up!" But even my pep talk wasn't working.

As I thought through a million excuses I could use to get out of our meeting, I was hit with the selfishness of my thoughts. God had given me the gift and opportunity to be a good friend, and here I was wanting to trade that in for some "me time" with a bag of Reese's and a spot on the couch. My friend was counting on me to show up, and God was reminding me of that simple truth.

It might seem silly or oversimplified, but showing up in life is more than half the battle. The Enemy wants us to run and hide. He wants us to take ourselves out of the game before we ever have a chance to play.

God placed you here on this earth to do great things, and sometimes, even when we don't want to in the moment, we need to show up. His Word encourages us, "Since we are surrounded by such a great cloud of witnesses, throw off everything that hinders and the sin that so easily entangles. And let us run with perseverance the race marked out for us" (Hebrews 12:1).

God has given you a race that nobody else can run. He has gifted you with abilities and opportunities totally unique to you. When I stopped to remember that, I grabbed my bag of Reese's and headed on to my friend's house. (Chocolate is always a good gift.)

Journal about a time you decided not to show up. What was your reason? Was it fear, worry, tiredness? The Enemy likes to keep us tangled up in some kind of mess that keeps us from showing up. But today, write yourself a pep talk that keeps you pressing on toward the finish line!

_____

_____

_____

_____

SEEKING HAPPINESS WHEN THE DAYS ARE HARD

Ever had a season that seemed to just take it out of you? I remember the weeks and months that followed God's revelation telling me to walk away from BlissDom, an international small business conference I ran. God had given me BlissDom during a time in life when I felt as if I had nothing to offer the world. It was a source of life and strength and hope. And here He was asking me to walk away from it.

Even though I knew leaving BlissDom was what God wanted me to do, it didn't make it any easier. Mark had retired from a great job to be at home with the boys, and BlissDom was what allowed us to do that. Now, Mark and I both were without a job, and we didn't know what was next. We were walking by faith, but I still felt paralyzed by fear and worry.

My struggle during this time reminded me of Jesus' disciples when they were caught in that storm on the Sea of Galilee. The waves were too big, the winds were too strong, and there was Jesus taking a nap in the boat. And when the disciples told Him they were doomed, Jesus simply told the storm to stop, and it did. The disciples were afraid of wind and water when the Maker of both was there with them.

It's easier to seek happiness when life is smooth, but when it's a season of life where things are difficult and we are just keeping our heads above water, seeking happiness can seem like nonsense. Know that even in the storm God is with you. He hasn't left you. He loves you and will see you through. Psalm 145 tells us, "The LORD is near to all who call on him" (v. 18). Fight to find your joy and stay close to Him, the bringer of all happiness, until the season of difficulty passes by.

For me and my family that meant that God had a better plan for us. He provided the next steps and led me to my next season working with a ministry, speaking, and writing. Had I not trusted and obeyed when things didn't make sense, in my disobedience I would have missed the future He had planned for me.

Write about a time when you were in a season of difficulty and God saw you through. Now, remind yourself that what He has done before, He will do again.

_____

_____

_____

THE COURAGE TO FORGIVE

Who was the last person to really hurt you? I'm talking about the kind of wound that sticks around long after the offense has occurred; a wound that doesn't go away, no matter how much you try to deal with it.

Most of us can identify who it was and exactly what was said. Our hurts and wounds possess an ability to stay with us, despite our best efforts to leave them behind.

But when we carry around those hurts, the anger that comes from those wounds festers and grows into a spirit of bitterness and offense. When our hearts become bitter and offended, we live life wounded and see every interaction through the lens of that pain.

So how can we be freed—fully freed—from the weight of our offenses and pain? We can choose to forgive and do for others what Jesus has done for us.

Forgiveness doesn't mean that the betrayal is okay.

It doesn't mean what the person did to you is okay.

Forgiveness is a gift to yourself, not a release of guilt to the offender.

It sets you free from the weight of carrying around all that hurt and anger. The book of Colossians tells us to "bear with each other and forgive one another if any of you has a grievance against someone. Forgive as the Lord forgave you" (3:13). Doesn't that sound good to your soul?

When we forgive others, we cast the burden of our wounds onto the One who received our stripes and bore our offenses.

Take a few minutes to pray about a hurt from someone. Pray and ask the Lord to give you the strength, courage, and peace to forgive. You may find it helps to pray, "Lord, I forgive (insert their name here). They don't owe me anything, not even an apology." It won't be easy, but it will be freeing.

_____

_____

_____

_____

GOD GIVES PAIN A PURPOSE

I couldn't believe it when our house went into foreclosure. *Foreclosure!* Mark lost his job, and then we lost it all. We had an expensive home, nice cars, and a comfortable lifestyle that all pointed to the fact that we had arrived. Yet little did we know that God would use this season of pain to loosen our hands off our sense of control so that we could find our joy in knowing our God is always in control.

The last thing we tend to think of when we are going through a painful storm in life is happiness. But when you have walked with Jesus long enough, you begin to learn that He will use the storm—and the growth that often comes with it—for your good in the next season.

My family and I lived as if our happiness were wrapped up in our material possessions, but God showed us that the opposite was true. When we lost it all, and all we had was each other and Him, we found true joy because our focus left material things and came back to Him and what He wanted for our lives.

Instead of staying focused on keeping up with the Joneses, we reconnected as a family and found real happiness.

Be comforted and know your pain always has a purpose. God's Word explains how one purpose for our pain is to be able to minister to others in their pain: "Praise be to the God and Father of our Lord Jesus Christ . . . who comforts us in all our troubles, so that we can comfort those in any trouble with the comfort we ourselves receive from God" (2 Corinthians 1:3–4).

Our happiness is based on our relationship with Jesus, and we can stand strong in the knowledge that He has a plan and will see us through any painful storms.

If you're in the middle of your storm, spend some time memorizing 2 Corinthians 1:3-4. Write it out here or in your journal. Once you have written it, write down what that verse means to you today. Then make a note to come back when this season has passed and record how God saw you through it.

_____

_____

_____

GETTING UNSTUCK

I have a low-level fear of getting stuck in an elevator. Every time the doors close, I wonder if this is finally the time that I end up stuck there forever, praying I have uneaten KIND bars in the bottom of my purse.

What scares me most about getting stuck in an elevator is that I would have no ability to do anything about it. I'd be at the mercy of others to get me unstuck.

The funny thing is, when I feel stuck in life, I feel just as powerless in those moments as I imagine I would feel in an elevator.

When it feels as if life isn't going anywhere, and there doesn't seem to be any movement in any direction, it can seem as if we're alone, and maybe just a little bit like God is nowhere to be found.

But the reality is that God is just as much with us in those moments when we feel stuck as He is when we feel like we're close to Him.

We all go through seasons when we feel stuck, when it feels as if our passion for God is waning and our growth in Him has stopped. It's in those times that we should draw the closest to God, asking for an extra measure of vision and passion from Him.

If you feel trapped, lost, adrift, or maybe just stagnant, know that God hasn't abandoned you but is at work in you to grow you closer to Him. Scripture affirms, "It is God who works in you to will and to act in order to fulfill his good purpose" (Philippians 2:13).

Are you in a place where you feel unable to move forward in your life? Spend some time asking the Lord to reveal to you how He's working in you. If you're not in that place, think about ways you can encourage others you might know who are.

_____

_____

_____

_____

_____

_____

"MY PEACE I GIVE TO YOU"

What comes to mind when you think of the word *peace*? Do you think of quiet scenes by a body of water? Do you think of treaties being signed? Do you think of conflict in your relationships being removed? Do you think of the all-too-brief moments after the kids have been put to bed? In all of these instances, peace exists, and yet, each example is only a part of what true peace is.

On the night Jesus was betrayed, He told His disciples about the true peace they had yet to experience. You would think that physically walking with Jesus would be enough to provide every ounce of peace they would ever need, but Jesus still intimated that there is an even deeper level of peace to know.

Even though the disciples would experience the same hate from the world that Jesus endured, they would be sustained by this peace that would go beyond any human ability to understand.

It's not a momentary peace that comes from this world, but an eternal peace given to us by God. He says in His Word, "I do not give to you as the world gives. Do not let your hearts be troubled and do not be afraid" (John 14:27). The kind of peace He gives us is the knowledge that no matter what happens on this earth, our eternity is secure in Him. And it's also the comfort of the Holy Spirit living in us. Through Jesus' death and resurrection, we have a peace that stands forever!

> If your heart feels troubled today (or the next time it does), try addressing God directly. Pray, "Lord, my heart feels troubled today. Will you show me Your peace in the midst of this pain and give me steps forward to walk in that peace?" Then sit silently before the Lord and allow His peace to comfort you.
>
> _____
>
> _____
>
> _____
>
> _____
>
> _____

IT'S NOT SUPPOSED TO BE THIS WAY

When something bad happens we often think, *It's not supposed to be this way, God.* And guess what? We're right. Things *aren't* the way they should be.

When God made the world there was peace, beauty, order, and goodness everywhere. But when Adam and Eve fell, they took all of creation down with them. Heartache, pain, suffering, death, loss, and grief all entered the world. Now when we look around us, we see its brokenness, and we long for what our souls remember of Paradise. The apostle Paul describes this longing in Romans 8: "We know that the whole creation has been groaning as in the pains of childbirth right up to the present time. Not only so, but we ourselves, who have the firstfruits of the Spirit, groan inwardly as we wait eagerly for our adoption to sonship, the redemption of our bodies" (vv. 22–23).

When we long for things to be different, we are joining the cry of creation as we groan together for God to make all things new. Though the statement, "It's not supposed to be this way," may be accurate in light of the fall, it's not helpful. In fact, it's a statement that can leave us feeling hopeless if we wallow in that mind-set for very long at all.

Instead of fighting against what is, let's release our expectations of what "should be" and ask, "Lord, how do You want me to respond? What do You want me to know? What do You want me to learn? How will You use this to strengthen me or to help others?" In asking the Lord what our next steps will be, we can move beyond what should have been and move toward hope and healing, and, ultimately, happiness.

What is something that has caused you to say, "Lord, it's not supposed to be this way"? Record that here or in your journal. Now ask the Lord the questions from above. As you record your answers, try not to overthink things, but just listen patiently for the Lord.

_____

_____

_____

_____

_____

GOD'S PLAN FOR YOUR LIFE IS A PROMISE OF GRACE

Jesus said, "Do *not* let your hearts be troubled" (John 14:27, emphasis mine). Easier said than done, right? Sometimes life's troubles seem to come at you in waves, and just when it feels as if you might catch your breath, you're hit by another one.

It was like that during a season when my husband, Mark, was very sick. I literally thought he would never get well. He'd see a new doctor, get a new medication, and things would look hopeful, only for a new wave of illness, a new symptom, a bad reaction to a medication, or some other terrible thing to take us down again.

Trust me when I tell you our hearts were troubled.

So how do we keep our happy heads above water when it seems as if we might drown? How do we follow Jesus' command to not let our hearts be troubled?

I have learned to do what David did when he was holed up in a cave, surrounded by his enemies. I strengthen myself in the Lord my God (1 Samuel 30:6). I remind myself that God's plan for my life is good, and then I pray a prayer of thanksgiving. I might say, "Lord, You know this thing has knocked me down, but I know You don't want me to live down here. You have a plan, and I'm excited about it. Give me the strength to get up, catch my breath, and move on."

Friend, God's plan for your life is a promise of grace. When your heart is troubled, cling to that promise.

Just as I have a mantra when my heart is troubled, try writing your own mantra (your truth talk) that you will speak over yourself when your heart is troubled.

_____

_____

_____

_____

_____

_____

REFLECTION

8

HEALTHY-HAPPY-WHOLE

Your health and happiness go hand in hand.

THE POWER OF A RECHARGE

I love my iPhone. There aren't many times during the day when it isn't within arm's reach. When the battery is low on my iPhone, the whole world stops until I get a recharge.

I'm that woman sitting on the floor in the middle of a busy airport waiting to recharge my precious iPhone!

It makes me wonder why I don't give myself that same priority.

God modeled a life rhythm of six days of work and a day of rest on the Sabbath. His Word explains His intentions for the Sabbath in Genesis: "By the seventh day God had finished the work he had been doing; so on the seventh day he rested from all his work. Then God blessed the seventh day and made it holy, because on it he rested from all the work of creating that he had done" (2:2–3). He designed us for cycles of work and rest. He even commanded that we remember the Sabbath to keep it holy. You would think one of the easiest of the Ten Commandments to follow would be to take a Sabbath, but most of us don't do it at all.

Getting enough rest on a weekly and daily basis helps us feel better and be happier.

When my life battery is getting low, I tend to make excuses for why I need to push myself to keep going. Friend, let's not do that this year. Your year of happiness is dependent upon you getting enough rest.

Today, give yourself permission to let something go, leave something undone, set something aside, and rest. As an act of accountability, at the end of today, come back to this page or to your journal and write down what you intentionally left undone so you would have time to rest.

_____

_____

_____

_____

_____

_____

TAKING PLAY SERIOUSLY

My dog, Mollie, is a golden retriever who doesn't retrieve. Her version of play is to snuggle, not to fetch. No matter how hard we have tried in the last eight years, that dog won't fetch, but she does take snuggling very seriously. It's her version of playtime.

We were all made with a need for some serious play. Researchers have proven that when children grow up without enough unstructured play it hurts their health, creativity, and even causes antisocial behavior.[1] For adults, play helps us de-stress, reduce anxiety, get creative, and feel happier.

Who decided that grown-ups aren't supposed to play? I think that over time, playtime gets pushed aside under the weight of responsibilities and heavy schedules. We feel as if play is something we only had the freedom to do as kids. So as adults it's easy for us to believe the lie that we are no longer entitled to time for play. But God's Word disputes this falsity when declaring, "The thief comes only to steal and kill and destroy; I came that they may have life; and have it abundantly" (John 10:10 NASB).

Think about your weekly schedule and then remember what you used to love as a child. Is there time built in to get seriously silly? Did you know that in the Old Testament God commanded the Israelites to celebrate and to have feasts (i.e., to party)? God knows our need for fun—He created the idea!

Make time in your schedule this week to play. You heard me right: put it on your calendar just like any important meeting, because it is important! Grab a friend and a board game, go play Frisbee with the kids, get your neighbors together for a game of charades, host your own living room Olympics—whatever sounds fun to you, do it!

_____

_____

_____

_____

_____

_____

THE IMPORTANCE OF SELF-CARE

There comes a time during every school year when my family's to-do list loses its mind. From sports practices, to rehearsals, to church events, to the growing mountain of laundry, it seems to *literally* pile on. When my to-do list starts its growth spurt, it isn't long before I start trading in my Whole30 recipes for an extra order of fries. And that's just the beginning.

Pretty soon I'm sleeping less, stressing more, doing fewer of the things I actually enjoy, and spending less and less time with Jesus. I'm so caught up in trying to care for everyone else's needs that I forget to give myself the same care.

Yet, taking care of ourselves physically (getting enough sleep, eating healthy food), emotionally (investing in our own happiness, avoiding negative self-talk), and spiritually (abiding in Jesus) is crucial for us to live the full, happy lives we are created for. We were made to help take care of others, but how can we do that if we aren't even caring for ourselves?

In 1 Corinthians 6:19–20, Paul says it like this: "Do you not know that your bodies are temples of the Holy Spirit, who is in you, whom you have received from God? You are not your own; you were bought at a price. Therefore honor God with your bodies."

The apostle Paul reminds us that our bodies are given to us so that we would worship God with them. He even goes so far to say our bodies are God's temple. When we care for ourselves, we're caring for the body God has given us to worship Him and serve others.

How can you practice self-care on a regular basis? Maybe it's something as simple as taking a nap on Sunday after church. Whatever it may be, take the next step and add self-care to your calendar or planner to make it official.

_____

_____

_____

_____

_____

BREATHING DEEPLY

I love movies. I go see almost every movie that comes out, especially the super-stressful, action-packed ones. When I go to these high-stress movies, I find myself glued to my seat, unable to move, with my eyes wide for most of the movie. Once the action dies down a bit, I realize that I've forgotten to breathe for who knows how long. I'm so stressed-out that I forget to breathe!

It's funny when it's fiction, but the same thing happens when I'm stressed in real life. When we are stressed or unhappy, we tend to hold our breath more or take quicker, more shallow breaths. Studies show that if we stop and take a breath while we're stressed, it actually helps to calm us and even lower our blood pressure. Even Navy Seals, one of the most elite special ops groups in the world, rely on basic breathing techniques to help them stay calm in the most stressful of situations.[1]

Learning to be aware of our breathing helps make sure we are getting enough oxygen and de-stressing, which leads to happiness!

It's no accident that God breathed life into us and then reminded us of that breath throughout Scripture. When we're stressed, we take our breath for granted and don't recognize where it comes from. The book of Job teaches us: "The Spirit of God has made me, and the breath of the Almighty gives me life" (33:4 NASB). By breathing deeply, we're giving ourselves a physical reminder of our dependence on God for our every need.

Take time today to become aware of your breathing and practice some deep breathing. You can start by breathing in while you count to four, hold it for two counts, and release your breath as you count to four. And while you breathe in deeply, let Job's words remind you where your breath comes from.

_____

_____

_____

_____

_____

LET YOURSELF REST

I was neck-deep in planning a women's conference and the deadlines for making final decisions for the schedule were quickly approaching. There were so many things to think through, so many details to consider, and so many decisions that seemed as if they all needed my input and approval. We were racing against the clock, and time was running out.

To be honest, I kind of loved the adrenaline and electricity of it all. It made me feel so alive to be doing something that felt so significant. But once the decisions were set and the plans made, the excitement of the season wore off, and I realized I was exhausted. Not tired. Exhausted. My body had been screaming at me to rest, but I couldn't slow down. If I slowed down, I might *miss* something. (Can I get an amen?)

God was telling me to rest. He wasn't telling me to take a break or a quick nap, but to take a real, true Sabbath rest. But of course, I didn't listen and the inevitable happened: I crashed. Hard. And let me tell you something, crashing *before* a conference is not good. It absolutely stole my joy and the happiness I should have been experiencing in a job well done.

God knows that we need a Sabbath, a deep day of holy rest. His

Word instructs us, "Remember the Sabbath day by keeping it holy" (Exodus 20:8). To keep something holy means to set it apart. To remember the Sabbath then means that we set apart a day each week when we stop from our work, just as God did from His. And when we rest as God intended, it reduces anxiety, increases happiness, and protects your body from illness.

If you normally do not take a Sabbath and rest, spend some time journaling today about how you can make room in your life for a Sabbath.

_____

_____

_____

_____

_____

_____

PROACTIVE, NOT REACTIVE

I am a planner. As a working mom with five sons with five different schedules, it's kind of a necessity that each and every day is planned out well in advance. If I lose control of even one small thing, it's like the anchor that keeps me grounded is loosed, and I end up at the mercy of whatever's next. I can always tell when I have let a busy life steal my happiness because I start becoming reactive, and trust me, "Reactive Alli" is not a happy person.

Just the other day, I had a problem with my Internet (something you can't plan for). Unfortunately, I had a deadline to meet that required my Internet to work, and I had no time to drive somewhere else to have access to Wi-Fi. I was stressed-out, and I'm embarrassed to say that the poor person at the Internet company got the full force of "Reactive Alli."

Maybe you can relate?

The thing is, my reactive self doesn't happen overnight. She creeps up on me slowly, and it's usually because I haven't taken care of myself. I haven't gotten enough sleep, I've eaten junk on the run, I haven't gotten any exercise, and I've allowed a very busy schedule to leave me rolling with the punches until eventually one of them lands.

Self-care doesn't mean we are being selfish. It means we are being proactive about carrying our own load in a way that honors God and others. Scripture tells us that "each one should carry their own load" (Galatians 6:5).

And when we do this well, our reactive selves don't have an opportunity to steal our happiness.

How can you start to spot your own
reactiveness and proactively respond?

_____

_____

_____

_____

_____

_____

FINDING YOUR PACE

I am often amazed at the pace of some people's lives. They can fix their families three actual meals a day, conquer an amazing workload, be at every kid's practice and performance, find time to exercise, and seemingly do it all with time to read the latest books. And here I am proud of the fact that I had extra time to shower today.

The reality is, most of us aren't wired like Wonder Woman, and we would be miserable if we tried to replicate her pace. But here's a great truth for us mere mortals: we don't have to live by anyone else's pace.

I have a friend who trained for and ran a marathon. She told me that at the beginning of the race she was running way too fast, competitively trying to keep up with the people around her. She knew if she kept up that pace, she would never finish the race. So she slowed down to the pace she'd trained at, and finished the race feeling great.

Though we might plan to do this and accomplish that, God invites us to find our pace in Him. When we trust Him to order our pace, we begin to live in step with His plans and purposes.

Stop for a second and consider this truth from Proverbs 16:9: "In their hearts humans plan their course, but the Lᴏʀᴅ establishes their steps." When we are secure in God's purpose for us, our pace reflects His peace.

If your life feels chaotic and out of control, perhaps you are running someone else's race. Spend some time today asking God to help you find your pace, then bravely lean into His purpose.

_____

_____

_____

_____

_____

_____

_____

GET SOME REST

As you've probably picked up on by now, I love watching movies. Sometimes, I love them so much that I don't pay attention to what time it is, or how late it's gotten. What I don't love, however, is waking up the next morning after one of those late nights.

My alarm seems to go off earlier than usual those days, and the coffee also seems to get brewed a little stronger than usual. You know what else is usual those days? My lack of happiness.

Let's face it, a sleep-deprived person is not a happy person. (And every mama of newborns said, "Amen!") There's a reason God rested on the seventh day of creation, and it wasn't because He needed a nap. Just as God created and called those things good, when He rested, He showed us that rest is just as good. His Word tells us, "In vain you rise early and stay up late, toiling for food to eat—for he grants sleep to those he loves" (Psalm 127:2). The extra strive is not necessary; God wants us to rest.

I don't know what keeps you up at night, but I do know that typically the next day, we regret the decision of having skipped getting the right amount of sleep. When we don't get enough rest, everyone around us pays the price.

As cheesy as it sounds, I set a timer on my phone to remind me to get ready for bed. That way, when I'm tempted to "pull an all-nighter" to accomplish some task or stay up late to finish binge-watching my favorite series, my alarm goes off and I say to myself, "Get some rest to be your best."

I know that a good night's sleep is as important to my happiness (and the happiness of those around me) as a weekly Sabbath is.

Tonight, set a timer on your phone to remind yourself to get ready for bed. Give yourself at least twenty minutes without your face in a screen before you lie down. You could take a warm bath or shower, pray, or relax, and then go through your mental gratitude list.

_____

_____

_____

_____

_____

REFLECTION

9

CHOOSING HAPPINESS

The choice really is yours.

CHOOSING TO BE HAPPY

You may have heard the old saying that we're all as happy as we make up our minds to be. It sounds trite, but it's great wisdom. You can make the decision to be happy, every single day, no matter your circumstances. So why aren't most of us living happier lives?

Think about it this way: you can tell yourself you are going to learn to knit all day long, read books about it, watch YouTube tutorials, but until you bust out the needles and yarn and decide to do it, it's just not going to happen. Until you make the decision to take the necessary steps toward accomplishing your goal, all it will ever be is a goal.

It's the same way with choosing to be happy. Sometimes all we need is to simply make the choice and ask God for vision, strength, and His perspective while living it out. Then we need to live in the freedom of this choice, taking the daily steps toward the happiness He provides.

In his search for life's meaning and purpose, King Solomon wrote, "I know that there is nothing better for people than to be happy and to do good while they live. That each of them may eat and drink, and find satisfaction in all their toil—this is the gift of God" (Ecclesiastes 3:12–13).

Do you notice what Solomon says is God's gift to man? The ability to *choose* to find satisfaction in the circumstances of life—to choose to be happy. When we choose happiness, we're choosing to find satisfaction in what God has already provided.

Today, when faced with the choice to be happy or not, be intentional about choosing happiness. Record your decision here or in your journal with the date and the circumstances surrounding your intentional choice.

_____

_____

_____

_____

_____

_____

_____

INVESTING IN YOUR FUTURE SELF

In ten years, I want to look back on the choices I make today and not regret them. I want the freedom not to weigh my future self down with today's choices. I want to invest in my future "happy Alli" by taking care of myself and loving those around me well. Also, I want a flying car so I can avoid airports, but that might be a little further down the road. But you know what I mean, right?

Think about just the last ten years of your life. Looking back, how many moments in those ten years do you wish you could have a redo for? If you're like me, there's probably a slide show of memories ready for your regretful viewing.

I could just kick myself for going to tanning beds when I was in high school. Every time I notice the skin on my neck getting suspiciously more loose, I want to go back in time and have a chat with sixteen-year-old Alli.

But what if it didn't have to be that way? Is there a way we can know which choices will help make our future selves happy? How can we begin to invest in our future selves?

God's Word has a thing or two to say about this. Proverbs 2:6 says, "The LORD gives wisdom; from his mouth come knowledge and understanding." If you want to start making your future self happy, start by making choices that are based on God's words, not man's.

When we start living by God's Word, we start living in step with the potential He's created us for.

We want to live up to all the potential God has placed inside us. So today, write out three things you can do this week that will make your future self happy. But don't just stop there—dig a little deeper and explain why you think those things will make your future self happy.

_____

_____

_____

_____

_____

GIVE YOUR DREAMS A GO

B ack in 2006, I first dreamed of writing a book, but I didn't know where to begin. So I did what most of us do in that situation—I Googled it. I discovered (according to Google) that unless I was famous, infamous, or well-connected, it was not going to happen. Later, I discovered the world of blogging, which helped me take a small step toward writing a book. Every blog post I wrote felt like a small step toward my dream, and each small step was preparing me to step into the reality of releasing my first book. I've seen it over and over again, but the biggest dreams are achieved one small step at a time!

Our God is a God of dreams, and I believe God plants dreams in us. Just as He gives us certain talents and gifts to pursue for His glory, He also gives us dreams to pursue a life that glorifies Him.

Think about what the apostle Paul says in Ephesians 2:10: "We are God's handiwork, created in Christ Jesus to do good works, which God prepared in advance for us to do." God has crafted our new lives in Jesus to be about the good works He has for us to do. When we walk in step with the dreams He's given us, we're walking in step with how

He's created us to live. God desires that our lives would be spent chasing after the dreams He has prepared for us!

If you have a dream that just won't go away, and that dream will in some way make the world a better place, start making plans to achieve it. Write out exactly what your dream is, then list out three small steps you can take to achieve it.

_____

_____

_____

_____

_____

_____

_____

_____

NOT TODAY, SATAN

If you're like me, it can feel easier to blame the Enemy when things start to go wrong in our world rather than take responsibility. But more often than not, the little things that go wrong in our day-to-day probably aren't from being under spiritual attack. (Hang with me here!) For example, when my iPhone battery dies or when my dog eats a pair of my favorite shoes, I can (most days) safely say the dog and my phone weren't working for the Devil in those moments.

But, if we're not on guard, the Enemy can use these small moments to steal our happiness and take our eyes off Jesus. (So maybe it *is* his fault!)

While we don't want to focus on our Enemy and blame everything on him, it doesn't do us any favors to forget that he is real and active in the world. And he is often trying to derail us with his trickery and misdirection.

Everyone has rough days. When I'm having a rough day, I try to remember it's not always spiritual attacks from the Enemy. However, when I sense him using my rough day to steal my joy, he's crossing a line and I tell him, "Not today, Satan." I even have a T-shirt that says it in big, white, block letters.

I love to put that shirt on and say that phrase out loud and remember that God has not given me a spirit of fear; but of power and love and a sound mind. It's a simple reminder that despite what happens today; I'm not going to give up or give in to the Enemy who has come to steal, kill, and destroy. Instead, I remember that God is with us to give us life to the full. Scripture tells us, "God gave us a spirit not of fear but of power and love and self-control" (2 Timothy 1:7 ESV). Embrace that today so you can approach life with courage.

Is there something you already do or could start doing that is a simple reminder to remember you are not going to let the Enemy steal your happiness?

_____

_____

_____

SOWING THE RIGHT SEEDS

I have a sincere fascination with watching things grow! The process of planting a seed and watching its slow transformation has always amazed me. But one thing that has never surprised me is the end result. Whatever kind of seed goes in the ground is exactly the type of plant that seed will eventually produce.

This is true of our lives as well. Check out what Paul says about this in 2 Corinthians 9:6: "Whoever sows sparingly will also reap sparingly, and whoever sows generously will also reap generously." We get out of life whatever we are willing to sow into it!

Where we are generous to sow the seeds that God has given us—whether in our finances, our talents, or our time—we will see those things eventually grow and reproduce in the lives of others.

We all have a choice of what seeds to sow in our lives and the lives of others. When we choose to sow seeds of peace and righteousness, we will eventually reap a harvest of happiness! And when we are generous to sow these seeds into the lives of others, our happiness increases as we watch the fruit of those things grow in them!

Spend some time asking God to show you what
seeds He's given you to plant. Then begin to
think through all the ways you can sow those
seeds in your life and in the lives of others.

_____

_____

_____

_____

_____

_____

_____

_____

_____

_____

DECIDING TO BE HAPPY EVEN WHEN YOU ARE A GROWN-UP

We all make lots of jokes about how hard it is to be a grown-up. We say things like, "I just can't adult today," as if *adult* is a verb. *Adulting* would include such fabulous things as paying bills, taking garbage out, scheduling and driving to appointments, replacing air filters, and flossing. But even with a life full of adulting, we can make the decision to squeeze all the happiness out of this life we can!

Deciding to be happy, even when you're getting your oil changed, is a choice to rejoice in the simple, even mundane, details of life. It's not seeing the glass as half-full or half-empty, it's being glad that you have a glass. (And yes, that you even get to put that glass in a dishwasher!) I've noticed this sense of joy in one of my sons. It's as if he truly takes delight in everything! Whether it's putting away his clean clothes (and making a zip line to do so) or feeding the dog, he has a zest for life that is amazing!

By choosing to be happy in our adult lives, we can reclaim some of that same childlike wonder and joy.

Paul reminds the Philippians to "Rejoice in the Lord always. I will say it again: Rejoice!" (Philippians 4:4). With all the pressures that come from adulting, we need to be reminded to rejoice in the simple things. Sometimes all it takes is making the decision to look for reasons to be happy!

Take time to write down just a few ways you can start deciding to be happy in the small, everyday things of life. In fact, today, practice saying, "Today, I am rejoicing that ____" and then fill in the blank! I wonder how many times you'll say you are rejoicing.

_____

_____

_____

_____

_____

_____

_____

THE REAL PURSUIT OF HAPPINESS

Every time I hear the story of Adam and Eve, it never fails to surprise me. Not surprised in the sense that I don't know what happens in the story, but surprised that they would make a choice to seek a happiness that they knew would lead to death. Remember, God said to them, "You must not eat from the tree of the knowledge of good and evil, for when you eat from it you will certainly die" (Genesis 2:17).

Let me tell you something; if God told me that drinking unfiltered tap water led to certain death, you'd better believe I'd be installing filters on every faucet! But despite God's warning, they decided to eat that fruit anyway.

And while I can joke about the water filter thing, the truth is, most of us make the same decision as our spiritual ancestors every day of our lives. While God has shown us the depths of His mercy, goodness, beauty, and life, we still often think that maybe there's something even better somewhere else.

We get caught up pursuing what we think will make us happy, when the Creator of all joy has offered us happiness as surely as if it were hanging from a tree.

Real happiness never comes from the pursuit of happiness, but instead from the beautiful provision of God. When we set our eyes on pursuing Him and His kingdom, He will provide depths of joy that sustain our happiness in Him through every season.

How have you pursued happiness instead of happily pursuing God? What "fruit" have you taken that you thought would provide you with lasting happiness? Know that no matter your past decisions, Jesus is longing for you to find your happiness in Him.

_____

_____

_____

_____

_____

_____

STOPPING THE SCROLL

Sometimes I'm not emotionally healthy enough to scroll through social media. I love all my friends, and I'm happy for the good times in their lives. But let's be real, if I'm up to my elbows in dishwater and disasters, the last thing I want to see are their highlight reels.

When the current experience of our lives doesn't seem to match up with the endless stream of lattes, lunches, and award ceremonies in our friends' lives, it creates a sense of discontent within us. In short, we end up jealous. Instead of being able to celebrate the good experiences of someone else, we end up comparing ourselves, and, ultimately, robbing ourselves of the joy of our own lives.

When that happens, the Enemy sneaks into our thoughts and begins to tell us the lie that our lives are miserable in comparison to the lives we see lived out on social media.

Our tendency toward comparison can keep us from being able to express gratitude to God for the good things we've been able to experience. This is why the book of Proverbs instructs, "Keep falsehood and lies far from me; give me neither poverty nor riches, but give me only my daily bread. Otherwise, I may have too much and disown you and say, 'Who is the LORD?' Or I may become poor and steal, and so dishonor the name of my God" (30:8–9).

It's okay to tell yourself, *Today, I'm going to invest in my happiness and stop the scroll.* When we do, we're choosing to invest in our own happiness now, rather than letting it be robbed by comparison.

Have you ever considered fasting from social media? What if you give yourself the freedom today to refrain from social media for seven full days? For those seven days, spend the time you would normally spend scrolling through social media to intentionally do things that make you happier.

_____

_____

_____

_____

JUST JUMP

Katie is a twenty-year survivor of breast cancer, and she celebrates life like no one I know. On the twentieth anniversary of being declared cancer free, she wanted to do something big. So she decided to jump out of an airplane.

I'm thinking I'd probably go more for a twenty-inch pizza, or twenty different scoops of Jeni's ice cream. Or maybe I'd watch twenty classic movies in a row. I can think of a lot of ways I'd celebrate such a big milestone; jumping out of a plane would not be one of them. I'd be too scared.

The thing I learned watching Katie live and celebrate life is that sometimes to move forward, we have to stand on the edge and jump.

If you're like me at all, sometimes when we stand at the edge of our next step and face our uncertain futures, fear tries to stop us.

But you know what I say to that? I say fear is a liar, because fear is not from God. The Enemy of our soul fights hardest when God is telling us to stand on the edge of our calling and to take a big giant leap of faith toward Him. God Himself tells us in the book of Joshua,

"Have I not commanded you? Be strong and courageous. Do not be afraid; do not be discouraged, for the LORD your God will be with you wherever you go" (1:9).

Because God has already overcome the Enemy of this world, I no longer have to fight fear. My faith will move me forward, even when fear tells me to freeze.

Today, take some time to remember God's faithfulness and let it redirect that fear that tries to keep you stuck. If it helps you, write down times you felt afraid but jumped anyway! Use these as inspiration to keep you moving forward.

_____

_____

_____

_____

_____

REFLECTION

10

THE POWER OF HAPPY WORDS

Let your words give life.

WOULD YOU TALK TO YOUR MAMA LIKE THAT?

Have you ever thought about how God created the world? Like, how He *actually* did it? Genesis tells us God spoke and life appeared. The Creator God formed words in His mouth and, literally, seas parted, land formed, and life sprang up from the ground.

As a mom, if I had one superpower, this would be it. I would speak and suddenly the laundry would be done, my schedule would be cleared, and my kids would obey every word I said. Life would be Eden.

And while we may not be superwomen (that's debatable), like God, our words have the power to create life.

In Ephesians 4:29, Paul encourages us by saying, "Do not let any unwholesome talk come out of your mouths, but only what is helpful for building others up according to their needs, that it may benefit those who listen."

His encouragement includes not only how we talk to (and about) others, but also how we talk to ourselves. It includes our inner dialogue, which, let's face it, is often not very life giving.

What would happen if you began to talk to yourself as kindly as you talk to others? As kindly as you talk to your mama? As kindly as Jesus would talk to you if He were sitting next to you? Ephesians tells us to say only what builds up. That includes the words you use on yourself.

Today, speak words of life over yourself. Begin by standing, facing a mirror, and saying five affirming, life-giving statements about yourself. Then, as the day provides you opportunity, speak words of encouragement over others as well. Record how you felt affirming yourself and how you felt encouraging others.

_____

_____

_____

_____

_____

BITING MY TONGUE

I can be *slightly* nitpicky about the most random things. I notice the small things, and it takes a lot for me not to point them out all the time, especially with my boys! Like when I ask them to clean their rooms, I hope they will look a certain way. (Let's be real . . . my expectations are high!) And even when it's good enough, there's still something in me that wants to show them the *right* way to do it.

When those nitpicky moments come, this verse from Proverbs 14:1 typically pops into my mind: "The wise woman builds her house, but with her own hands the foolish one tears hers down." Though we may feel as if we're helping when we point out the flaws of our family, we're often making unnecessary critiques. Instead of building up our families with words of affirmation, we're tearing down the happiness of our home, brick by brick, with each unnecessary criticism.

I've learned that if it isn't *absolutely necessary* to their survival, it's best to let a critical thought flow right in and out of my mind. Though it may feel as if we absolutely need to tell our family our every thought, aren't our words used best when we speak life into our family? Let's use our words to build up and nurture the families God has given us.

But we can't just stop with biting our tongues. We also have to practice speaking positive words over our family and others. The more positively we speak to others, the more our brains secrete serotonin, the happy hormone. The more serotonin our brains produce, the happier we feel, the more we are likely to speak positively to those around us, and so on and so on and so on.[1]

Of course, we can't walk around pretending everything around us is perfect. It's a fact of life that sometimes we have to point out what's not right so it can get better. We just want to make sure our critical eye doesn't become a critical spirit, and in turn, a critical mouth.

Ask God to show you if there are ways you accidentally use your words to tear down the happiness of your own home. How can you change that habit to give your family members a happier home environment?

_____

_____

_____

BUILDING EACH OTHER UP

When was the last time you went through a hard season in life, when it seemed as if wave after wave of difficulty came at you? What was helpful to you during that time? When it seemed as if life's troubles were relentless, was it helpful knowing you had someone who had your back, encouraging you each step of the way?

In Ephesians 4, Paul says that when we encourage each other and "[speak] the truth in love," (v. 15) we are like a body who "builds itself up in love, as each part does its work" (vv. 15–16).

We are designed to build each other up, restoring each other in love. Not only do our words have the potential to restore others to happiness, but we also receive joy ourselves when we encourage others, just as much as if we were the ones getting the encouragement.

Words of affirmation and encouragement are tools that have the power to undo the damage that life inflicts on us and others. Even the simplest of encouragements can be what helps us get through some of life's more difficult seasons. By speaking the truth in love, we are restoring each other back to the happiness that God desires for us.

Pray and ask the Lord to call to mind someone
you can encourage this week. Don't overthink it
or let it become a big talk that seems hard to do.
Encouragement can be done in the smallest of ways.
Maybe it's paying for the coffee of the car behind you
in the drive-through line, or sending an intentional
text to let a friend know you are thinking of them.

HOW GOD BUILDS US UP

It was late Friday afternoon, and I wasn't nearly done with all that I needed to do. It was one of those weeks with multiple deadlines, and after all my attempts at trying to prioritize, schedule, and plan, the hours just weren't adding up. I sat slumped at my kitchen table and couldn't believe that I had let this happen. I proceeded to spend the better part of the day beating myself up, feeding myself the same tired lines, "Maybe I'm not good enough to do this. Maybe I'll never be good enough."

In the five days since Monday, I went from being totally confident in what God was doing through me to totally defeated because of the lies of the Enemy.

The lies of the Enemy will always seek to tear us down, but the truth of God's grace will always seek to build us up. No one is ever motivated to do better by criticism or shaming—that's not the heart of God. But that's often what we do to ourselves, isn't it?

We say, "I'll never be enough." But Jesus says, "I'm more than enough." We say, "I can't carry this." But Jesus says, "Let Me carry it for you." Jesus looks at us in our failures and mistakes and doesn't cast the first stone, but gives us grace upon grace.

When you're tempted to beat yourself up over your mistakes, choose to treat yourself the way Jesus treats you—with love and grace. The book of Ephesians encourages us with these words: "To each one of us grace has been given as Christ apportioned it" (4:7).

Practice self-compassion, not self-criticism. Happiness comes when we offer (ourselves) grace just as Jesus does.

Think of a situation in which you could have chosen godly self-compassion over ungodly self-criticism. What steps can you take to be more compassionate with yourself in the future?

_____

_____

_____

_____

TALK ABOUT YOURSELF IN A MANNER WORTHY OF YOU

As a business consultant, I listen to people talk about themselves all the time, and a lot of the time it isn't the good stuff. People will come to me with everything going wrong in their business, which often translates to what's going wrong with them.

It's as if there's this mythical level of success that, until they reach it (whatever "it" is for them), they can't be satisfied in the work they've already accomplished. By their own words and attitudes, they become their own worst enemy to their success.

Does that feel familiar? You don't have to be a business owner to feel this! Even in the most regular daily life, we can become our own worst enemy because of what we choose to say about ourselves. Needless to say, this wreaks havoc on our happiness!

Jesus says our mouths speak out of the overflow of our hearts (Luke 6:45), and when we talk about ourselves to others, what we really believe about ourselves is revealed. If we truly believe that we are His workmanship and are loved by our Father, our words will reflect that truth, both to ourselves and to others.

The Lord has done a great work in you. Don't let your own mouth be a tool the Enemy can use against you to steal your happiness and confidence. You are fearfully and wonderfully made—created in God's image!

Stand in front of your mirror and say every nice thing you can say about yourself. Go ahead and have some fun with it! God is even more fond of you than you are! You can't out-love God.

_____

_____

_____

_____

_____

_____

_____

THE POWER OF OUR WORDS

God has consistently used the encouraging and affirming words of others to speak peace to the storms that have raged during the hardest moments of my life. More than a change in my circumstances, the life-giving words of others have served as a bedrock that the Lord has used to help me stand on Him.

Even though our words contain the power to create life, they also possess the ability to destroy everything in their path. Like a wildfire, words can cause damage we never intended and leave scars that take years to heal. We grow up hearing that "sticks and stones may break our bones, but words can never hurt us," but most of us (if not all of us), carry memories that prove the old cliché wrong.

Our words are powerful. Scripture says, "The mouth of the righteous is a fountain of life" (Proverbs 10:11).

If we want to experience the happiness that God intended for us and others, it often begins with the words we choose to say.

Our words are meant to build up those around us and can serve to heal the damage others have carried. You never know how God could use your words of encouragement to bring healing to the destruction caused by the words of others. When we speak life-giving words of affirmation and encouragement, we are building each other up in love, word by word.

Write just one thing that you can say to someone
that will build them up. Then tell them! It
could be the healing they're waiting for.

_____

_____

_____

_____

_____

_____

_____

TRUTH TALK

My mama used to say, "You are what you eat." I feel certain that is not true, because if it were, I'd be wrapped in a candy wrapper, covered in chocolate, and filled with peanut butter. (Heaven knows I love me some Reese's Peanut Butter Cups.)

When computers were first becoming a thing, they had a similar expression they used to describe problems that came up in the software. The expression was "garbage in, garbage out." (I mentioned it earlier!)

Both expressions basically mean the same thing. If you feed the computer's brain garbage, it is going to give you garbage right back. If all I ever feed myself is junk, I'll get the results of a junky diet.

The same is true of our hearts, minds, and spirits. If we feed ourselves a steady diet of negativity, guilt, shame, and lies . . . that's what we will get in return. "For the mouth speaks what the heart is full of" (Matthew 12:34).

Garbage in, garbage out. Goodness in, goodness out.

We have to fill our minds with the right things; things that are positive, that give us life, that teach us to forgive, that show us how to love and have grace for others. We need a steady diet of God's Word so that when any negative words, thoughts, or actions are hurled our way, we can extinguish them with truth.

Today, write down any negative things you have believed about yourself. Then cross them off and replace them with a truth from God's Word.

_____

_____

_____

_____

_____

_____

_____

_____

REFLECTION

_____

_____

_____

_____

_____

_____

_____

_____

_____

_____

_____

_____

11

A HAPPY HEART IS GOOD MEDICINE

Your heart is yearning for some happy.

PROTECTING YOURSELF FROM THE CURSE OF COMPARISON

The Olympics are the peak of athletic competition in the world. People train from childhood for a chance to compete. The ceremony at the end of each competition, with medalists standing on the podium receiving gold, silver, and bronze medals, is the pinnacle of athletic achievement.

Scientists decided to study the happiness level of the three athletes who get to stand on that podium and discovered the happiest medalists are those who take home the gold (of course) and the bronze. In fact, the bronze medalist is consistently happier than the silver, even though the silver medalist did a better job than the bronze medalist.[1]

Silver medalists compared themselves to the gold medalists and felt disappointed. But the bronze medalists compared themselves to the athletes who didn't get a medal at all, and they felt grateful to be on the podium.

When are times in your life when you've felt like the silver medalist? Was it when someone else got the promotion? Was it when your friend got the house that you've always wanted? Was it when you saw your friends' lives on social media? Truth is, we're at our worst when we let comparison get the best of us.

Now, think about the times you've been the happiest. Were they centered around accomplishments or possessions? Chances are, no. At least, not for long. We are at our happiest when we feel deeply grateful for what God has given us. The book of Proverbs declares, "The blessing of the LORD brings wealth, without painful toil for it" (10:22).

We were created to find our happiness in Him, no matter the circumstances of our lives. Journal about a time when you let comparison steal your contentment. Draw a picture of a bronze medal as a reminder to be content, and then ask Jesus to give you the simple joy of a contented heart.

_____

_____

_____

_____

THE WONDER OF WORSHIP

I love to sing worship songs. Like, a lot a lot. If God had given me my choice of natural gifts and abilities, I'd have been one heck of a worship leader. But apparently the Lord had other plans for me! However, my lack of natural musical ability doesn't keep me from singing—and for good reason too. Did you know the Bible commands us (more than fifty times to be exact) to worship Him through song?

We were created to be worshipers. We were made to see His goodness, to experience His presence, and to echo back to Him His majesty. The book of Psalms tells us to "sing praises to God, sing praises; sing praises to our King, sing praises" (47:6). When we sing to Him in worship, we are reminding ourselves of who God is and what He's done for us.

God has given us a mutually beneficial gift in worship. He loves to be worshiped, and He created us to find joy in worship because it's there that we often feel His nearness. In His nearness, we see and feel His love, His grace, His mercy, His majesty, and His beauty.

Singing songs of worship has helped me savor the good days and has been a source of comfort and peace in my hardest days. When we worship as an intentional act of praise, we can have peace amid any storm because we can see the One who reigns over the storm!

Today's action step is simple: sing your heart out and enjoy the happiness that comes with it! Roll down the windows and crank up the radio, or pick a playlist on your phone and belt out your favorite songs.

_____

_____

_____

_____

_____

_____

_____

GIVING FOR JOY

Science proves that giving makes us happier people. Researchers used MRI technology to show that when we help and give to others, we engage the same parts of our brain as when we eat food or have sex.[1] That's powerful stuff right there.

It's funny to me how scientists need to work for years only to prove the truth that Jesus taught two thousand years ago.

Think about it for a moment: your happiness has less to do with how much you have and more to do with how much you give. Our brains are wired to experience the same satisfaction when eating an incredible meal as when we're generous!

I love the example that the apostle Paul gives us of what living generously looks like. In the book of Acts, Paul was preparing to leave the new church plant in Ephesus, and he gave them this last encouragement: "In everything I did, I showed you that by this kind of hard work we must help the weak, remembering the words the Lord Jesus himself said: 'It is more blessed to give than to receive'" (Acts 20:35).

Paul spent most of his life giving as much of himself away as possible.

He knew the simple truth of Jesus' words and knew that his life would be best spent living out of the generosity he had been given in Jesus.

When we live generously, we're living in step with how God made us. List three ways you can begin to live more generously. If you want a bigger challenge, list three people, charities, or church ministries that you can begin to give to.

_____

_____

_____

_____

_____

_____

_____

STACKING STONES
OF REMEMBRANCE

I love holding onto things that remind me of important times in my life. Be it a picture, a trinket, or a letter, I've collected these small tokens to remind me of what life was like then. Every now and then I'll pass by one of these things, and I am filled with gratitude toward God for allowing me to have such rich memories. Memories of times He has seen me through a particularly painful season of life, or when I've celebrated a victory, or when He has faithfully reminded me of His presence.

The Israelites did this too. When Joshua led God's people to Canaan, they had to pass through the Jordan River, which flooded at that time of year. There was no way around it; yet, God had a plan. Just as God parted the Red Sea, so He stopped up the waters of the Jordan and the Israelites passed through the river on dry ground.

Once they were on the other side, God told them to find a man from each of the twelve tribes. He then told them, "Go over before the ark of the LORD your God into the middle of the Jordan. Each of you is to take up a stone on his shoulder, according to the number of the tribes of the Israelites, to serve as a sign among you" (Joshua 4:5–6).

The Israelites were commanded to stack these stones as a reminder of God's goodness toward them.

Just as God told the Hebrew people to stack stones of remembrance so they would always remember His provision, we need to stack our own stones for all the ways that God has been good to us.

Remembering His goodness is an investment in our own happiness!

You don't have to literally stack up stones to remember God's goodness, but you can if you want to! I surround myself with my happy memory souvenirs. I have a friend who writes down her memories and keeps them in a jar. What are some ways you can be intentional about remembering God's goodness?

_____

_____

_____

_____

WHAT WOULD YOU DO FOR FREE?

There was a time in my life when it seemed as if every waking hour of every day was spent taking care of the house and keeping the children fed, out of trouble, and reasonably well-behaved. I knew both hobbies and passions brought happiness in life, but there was simply no time to pursue my hobbies, and I had no energy to even think about developing my passions

Where do you even start when you're functioning as an empty cup? For me, I started asking myself, "If money and time were no limitation, what would I do with my life?" After my dreams of lying on a beach forever subsided, I thought about what it would be like to be able to pour into the lives of thousands of women, encouraging them to be exactly who God had called them to be.

Slowly, over time, my passionless, empty cup began to be filled with the dreams God started to give me. And He miraculously gave me the energy to start to pursue them one small step at a time. I knew that even if I never saw a cent from pursuing those passions, it was still a dream worth chasing. Psalm 37 states, "Take delight in the LORD, and he will give you the desires of your heart" (v. 4).

At a time when I felt stuck, the question, "What would you do for free?" helped clarify what I was truly passionate about. And when we can clearly identify our dreams, we can begin to take the next steps necessary to start to see them go from dreams to reality.

> What would you do for free? What is something
> you're so passionate about that you would pursue
> it even if no one ever paid you to do it? Now spend
> some moments in prayer asking God to show you
> some next steps to accomplish this dream.
>
> _____
>
> _____
>
> _____
>
> _____
>
> _____
>
> _____

THE POWER OF MUSIC

When my boys leave for school, I play worship music so loudly and sing so badly, our dog Mollie has been known to hide behind the couch. (Ouch.)

Despite her criticism, it's still one of my favorite moments of the day because I'm able to completely and freely express my love for Jesus as loudly as I can in that moment.

God made us to be vibrant and expressive worshipers of Him. He knows that when we unashamedly praise Him with reckless abandon, we're plugging into how He designed us to be and we will experience the joy that only comes from joyfully worshiping Him. David knew this truth intimately and modeled for the rest of Israel what a deep, thriving life of worship looked like, both in the highs and lows. One of David's psalms encourages us to, "Worship the Lord with gladness; come before him with joyful songs" (100:2).

Even the secular world has started to tune into what we and David know, that simply listening to positive music can help boost our mood. If that's true, think about the happiness in store for us when we participate and sing along to music that reminds us of our identity and purpose!

What are five songs that make you happier? Make a
playlist and start adding them to your day, every day!

_____

_____

_____

_____

_____

_____

_____

_____

_____

_____

_____

GENEROSITY IS THE GIFT THAT KEEPS GIVING

In 2013, researchers from the University of Wisconsin discovered this profound truth: helping others makes us happier. (*Gasp!*) Results were gathered from a sixty-year study that tracked ten thousand 1957 Wisconsin high school graduates throughout their lives. The study showed that those who said helping others was important in their mid-thirties ended up being happier thirty years later.[1]

As obvious as this discovery is, it only proves what God has told us in His Word. Almost three thousand years ago, King Solomon said what scientists are just now coming around to: "A generous person will prosper; whoever refreshes others will be refreshed" (Proverbs 11:25). When we live lives generous to those around us, we are investing just as much in their happiness as we are our own happiness.

After all, we are created in the image of God who delights to act generously. God has generously given us everything we have and loves to lavish on us what will help us grow in Him. Our happiness in helping others reflects God's happiness in helping us.

When was the last time you remember being intentionally generous toward someone? Is it a way of life for you, or something you have to think about doing? In what ways would you like to change this about yourself?

_____

_____

_____

_____

_____

_____

_____

_____

_____

REFLECTION

_____

_____

_____

_____

_____

_____

_____

_____

_____

_____

_____

_____

12

BUILDING A HAPPY LIFE

Being intentional with the details brings ease.

OH, HOW FAR YOU'VE COME

Belinda, a stay-at-home-mom friend of mine, dropped out of college shortly after she was married. Although she always wanted to go back, the kids started coming, and well, life happened, and she never went back.

Each time she thought about it, she'd make a plan and say, "If I started now, I'd be finished by such-and-such a year." Then, sure enough, that year would come and go, and she wouldn't have even started the process. When she thought about the four-year commitment involved, the finish line felt so far away that she just never started.

One day when we were talking, I asked her why she kept putting it off. She said the idea of something that was going to take her four years to finish was just too overwhelming. I suggested she just start by taking one class. So she started by taking that one class. Then the next semester she took three classes, and then she became a full-time student. Three years later she graduated and now teaches first grade, a job that she loves and that matches her kids' schedule as well!

When we have a big goal, it's easy to focus on how far we have to go instead of focusing on one step at a time. God's Word supports this notion in Zechariah: "Who dares despise the day of small things, since the seven eyes of the Lᴏʀᴅ that range throughout the earth will rejoice when they see the chosen capstone in the hand of Zerubbabel?" (4:10).

I mean, when my goal is losing five pounds to fit in my jeans again, it seems as if it will take years! But instead of staying focused on how much more work is ahead or how long it will take, I choose to focus on how far I've come. I promise you, when I focus on the pound I've lost instead of the four I still have to lose, it motivates me to keep going.

Think about the creation. The Lord could have spoken into existence in one moment, but He took six days. He took his time celebrating the process every step of the way! And likewise, we should too!

What is a goal you have been putting off because it's too overwhelming to think about starting? Write down your goal, break it down into small steps that you can more easily accomplish, and then . . . start!

_____

_____

GOING FOR A QUICK WIN

As I work with business owners and people who are starting their first business, I look for ways to help them get a quick win early on. Starting something new or learning new skills can be a very difficult task. I have found that a quick win provides immediate motivation to plow through, even when the project seems very challenging.

I've also learned that the strategy of a quick win helps in so many areas of life. This is especially true when we are feeling overwhelmed by large tasks and responsibilities. If you are feeling the weight of having "so much to do," look for the small tasks that are part of your big projects and go for a quick win with those.

Have you ever noticed that simple act of crossing something off our to-do list makes us feel more accomplished and happier? But when we sit around fretting about all that has to be done (accomplishing nothing) our happiness starts to take a nosedive?

Think about what Solomon writes in Proverbs 12:11: "Those who work their land will have abundant food, but those who chase fantasies have no sense." Solomon gets it and tells us that to enjoy the benefits of the harvest, we have to actually start with the soil. We have to get moving and accomplish something, even when the task is large!

We can't simply wish for food. At some point we have to pick up the plow and get to work on the task in front of us. When you're looking at a new or challenging task, find the quick win and think about the first few small steps you can take.

Write out the steps for a project that feels overwhelming to you right now. Then choose your quick win. Crossing a couple of small tasks off your list will feel so great!

_____

_____

_____

_____

_____

_____

INTENTIONAL SOCIAL MEDIA

You know the story. You're at the end of your bedtime routine, lying in bed, and there you are, phone in hand, endlessly scrolling to catch up on the day's events on your newsfeed. After a while, maybe some of these thoughts cross your mind:

How long have I been looking at this thing?

I wonder what Angela from third grade is up to?

Ooh, an article with "37 Adorable Pictures of Baby Goats!"

Guess I'll scroll through this one *last article.*

Six articles later, you realize it's midnight, hurriedly set your alarm, and finally go to bed.

We live in an age when we are more connected than ever before. For the first time in history, we can know what our friends are doing without even having to ask them. But if we're more connected than ever, why do we feel more disconnected than ever before?

Study after study has come out in recent years that shows the more time we spend on social media, the less happy we are.[1] I've certainly seen that in my life! But even though I've felt discontented and discouraged when scrolling mindlessly, I do believe we can use social media and protect our happiness *if we do it intentionally.* For me, I limit my total social media time every day to thirty minutes. Instead of scrolling passively through my feed, I find that when I'm intentional about using my social media to connect with others (sending direct messages of encouragement or commenting on statuses in genuine, heartfelt ways), it can be a great source of encouragement both for me and my friends.

God has given us an incredible means to connect with and encourage others. Social media, like anything else in this world, has the power to be incredibly good, if we are thoughtful about how we let it be a part of our lives. The book of Colossians puts this into context by saying, "Whatever you do, whether in word or deed, do it all in the name of the Lord Jesus, giving thanks to God the Father through him" (3:17).

> God has given us an incredible means to connect with others. Write down three ways you can use your social media accounts to encourage others.
>
> _____
>
> _____
>
> _____

DELEGATING THE DRUDGERY

I read an article recently that said researchers found that one way people can increase their happiness in their daily life is by hiring people to do the tasks they don't like to do.

Essentially, if we have the extra budget to pay somebody to pull those weeds or to mow the lawn or clean the house, we will feel less stressed by those tasks and in turn feel happier. Even though it might cost a little bit extra out of our pockets, the return on our happiness can be well worth the expense of delegating the tasks.

That sounds nice, right? Well, I don't know about you, but I can't always just hire someone to do the cleaning and the yardwork. But my husband and I do have five sons, so we've delegated all the housework drudgery to the boys! Happy!

While reading the article, I couldn't help but think of Moses. Moses was a guy who felt as if he had to do it all. So when Moses first brought the Israelites out of Egypt, he sat with them all day trying to handle everyone's problems. But when his father-in-law Jethro saw this, Jethro came to Moses and said, "What you are doing is not good. You and these people who come to you will only wear yourselves out. The work is too heavy for you; you cannot handle it alone" (Exodus 18:17–18). Jethro reminded Moses to delegate his tasks so he could focus on what he was meant to do.

Like Moses, we weren't meant to do it all. When we find ourselves trying to get through the drudgery, it usually comes at the expense of our happiness. I have friends who actually swap out things in their lives they hate to do. One hates to run carpool, and the other hates to do homework with their kids, so they swap! They're each happier because they aren't stuck doing things they hate and they get to do things they enjoy. And that happiness carries over to the rest of their family.

What are the top three tasks that are drudgery for you? Then list out ways you can delegate that drudgery. Even if you don't have the budget for it, be creative and think of some ways to get it off your plate. You'll be happier for it!

_____

_____

_____

A WISE WOMAN BUILDS HER HOUSE

Every once in a while, I feel myself getting frustrated at the kids or my husband, and at that point where I'm just about to lose it with them, the Lord often brings a verse to my mind. "The wise woman builds her house, but with her own hands the foolish one tears hers down" (Proverbs 14:1). That verse serves as my plumb line to remind me that as the woman of the house (in my case the *only* woman of the house), I can set the emotional tone.

I have a choice in that moment to let my frustration flow and upset everybody else in house (essentially tearing my house down). Or, I can use self-control by dealing with my own frustrations and keep building my house the way God desires for me to.

A wise woman builds her house with wisdom, with knowledge, and with extra strength from the Holy Spirit. There are a million reasons every day to get frustrated. A wise woman knows the difference between a minor inconvenience that can be overlooked for the sake of the family's happiness and peace, and a serious issue that needs to be addressed. Wise women don't major in the minors.

When the frustration comes (and believe me, it will!), what you do with that frustration can result in either adding life and peace to your family or taking it away.

Let's be women who are wise in our words and actions!

Take time today and find rest knowing that God can always build back up what we've torn down. Then, spend time in prayer asking Him to help you remember to be a woman who chooses to build her house.

_____

_____

_____

_____

_____

_____

_____

STARTING WELL

Because I'm not naturally a morning person, I set myself up for success the night before. The coffee is ready to brew, the little kids' school clothes are all laid out for them, and I take care of any small things that need to be done first thing in the morning. (This could be a permission slip for a field trip, a check I need to write, etc.)

If I don't set myself up for success the night before, my mornings are chaotic and hurried, and everyone starts their day a frazzled mess. That's a terrible way to start the day.

We each have parts of our day that are our trigger points. A friend of mine thinks the perfect end to any day is a warm bath and soft candlelight. But all too often she goes into her master bathroom at the end of the day to discover that her daughter's toys, hair accessories, and clothing are strewn everywhere. It pushes every button she has.

So what did she do? She created an organized spot in her master closet for the hair supplies, a place under the sink for the bathtub toys, and a hamper for the clothes. After just a couple of days with the new system, she was enjoying the peace and tranquility at the end of the day she needed. She was modeling what the book of Proverbs says a woman of noble character looks like: "She watches over the affairs of her household and does not eat the bread of idleness" (31:27).

Sometimes the key to happiness is a little (or a lot) of organization. Take the time to do the small things that you know will reduce your stress. You'll be astounded by how much better it makes your life!

What can you do to set yourself up for less stress and more happiness each day? Write down one or two small things you can do today to get started.

_____

_____

_____

_____

_____

_____

WHAT REAL
SUCCESS LOOKS LIKE

Someone once asked me how I wanted to be remembered. I said, "You mean, like at my funeral?" She laughed and said, "Well not exactly, but yes, sort of. After you are gone, what do you want people to say about who you were as a person?"

The answer was easy. I said, "I want people to say that I was a woman who obeyed God and that I loved others well."

In the business world, success is measured by how effectively you reach your goals. I think the same can be true of life. But our life goals cannot be measured by wealth and fame, because I don't know of anyone who would want to be remembered solely for the amount of money they had in the bank. God's Word reminds us of what a path to a flourishing life looks like: "Keep this Book of the Law always on your lips; meditate on it day and night, so that you may be careful to do everything written in it. Then you will be prosperous and successful" (Joshua 1:8).

Most people want their lives to count for something. They want to make a difference in the world. They want to know they have a purpose, and they want to be successful at living out that purpose.

To me, success is obeying God in all things. It means being faithful to take care of the things God has entrusted to me—namely, my husband, my children, my family, my calling, and the precious friends He has given me for this lifetime. If I get that right, then I think people will say I obeyed God and that I loved others well. And that, my friends, is my definition of success.

> What does success look like to you? Write down how you want to be remembered, and then make that the goal by which you measure your success.
>
> _____
>
> _____
>
> _____
>
> _____
>
> _____
>
> _____

FINISH WELL

Ever heard the phrase, "Finish well"? This little phrase has helped me so many times. It's this bite-sized encouragement that reminds me it doesn't matter how my day started—I always have the ability to finish well. When I hear it, I get this image of a runner who stumbles when the starting pistol fires, but instead of giving up, she gets her feet under her and refocuses on the finish line ahead.

If you're like me, it's too easy to focus on what's gone wrong throughout a day. A missed deadline, a bad hair day, forgetting to charge your phone the night before (can I get an amen?). If we're not careful, any of these things have this crazy ability to draw our attention away from the goals that God has for us today.

We get tripped up on our past mistakes and forget the joy found in pursuing God's purpose in our lives.

But remember: the past doesn't define you; it refines you and makes you stronger.

The apostle Paul had this same attitude. In Philippians 3:13–14, he writes, "One thing I do: Forgetting what is behind and straining torward what is ahead, I press on toward the goal to win the prize for which God has called me heavenward in Christ Jesus."

Paul's encouragement to the Philippians—and to us—was to follow his example and not fixate on the past but instead press on toward Jesus to finish their race well.

What is the race God has given you to run? Let's set our eyes on the prize God has for us in Christ and finish well. That is where real happiness lies.

_____

_____

_____

_____

_____

_____

_____

GRATITUDE

My Savior—

Thank You, Jesus, for life, meaning, and real happiness. You are everything.

My family and friends—

Mark, thank you for your relentless pursuit of holy happiness with me no matter what life throws our way. Your steadfast support and belief in me, in us, and our calling gives me so much strength. I love you.

Justin, Jack, Joey, James, and Jeremiah, nothing this side of heaven makes me happier than being your mom, enjoying every day with you and all the years of craziness and laughter. Y'all have my heart and you make me so proud.

Carol, thank you for holding my arms up when I got weak. Thank you for hours of wrestling through happiness with me and helping me find just the right words to explain what was in my heart.

My colleagues—

Thank you, Laura Minchew, Carly Kellerman, Adria Haley, and the entire team at HarperCollins Christian Publishing for your heart, brilliance, and vision. Thank you, Jenni Burke, for your love and amazing work.

My new friends—

Thank you for taking the challenge and joining me on this mission to find holy happiness. My prayer and hope for you is that these words help you find happiness in this crazy world.

NOTES

HAPPY ROOTS
1. Sue Shellenbarger, "The Power of the Doodle: Improve Your Focus and Your Memory," *Wall Street Journal*, July 29, 2014, https://www.wsj.com/articles/the-power-of-the -doodle-improve-your-focus-and-memory-1406675744.

HAPPINESS IS A WORTHY GOAL
1. John Piper, "God Is Most Glorified in Us When We Are Most Satisfied in Him," desiringgod.org, October 13, 2012, https://www.desiringgod.org/messages/god-is -most-glorified-in-us-when-we-are-most-satisfied-in-him.

TAKE A STEP TOWARD YOUR PASSION
1. Vivek Wadhwa, "The Case for Old Entrepreneurs," *Washington Post*, December 2, 2011, https://www.washingtonpost.com/national/on-innovations/the-case-for-old -entrepreneurs/2011/12/02/gIQAulJ3KO_story.html?utm_term=.2d53bea9987f.
2. Library of Congress, "Benjamin Franklin and Electricity," *America's Story from America's Library*, accessed January 10, 2018, http://www.americaslibrary.gov/aa /franklinb/aa_franklinb_electric_1.html.
3. Bill Murphy, Jr., "14 Inspiring People Who Found Crazy Success Later in Life," Inc. com, March 24, 2015, https://www.inc.com/bill-murphy-jr/14-inspiring-people-who -found-crazy-success-later-in-life.html.

4. Wayne G. Hammond, "J.R.R. Tolkien," *Encyclopædia Britannica*, November 23, 2017, https://www.britannica.com/biography/J-R-R-Tolkien.

YOUR FAVORITE FIVE
1. Jim Rohn, Jim Rohn.com, https://www.jimrohn.com/.

THE $133,000 RAISE?
1. Eric Barker, "Happy Thoughts: Here Are the Things Proven to Make You Happier," *Time*, April 4, 2014, http://time.com/49947/happy-thoughts-here-are-the-things -proven-to-make-you-happier/.

THE DISCIPLINE OF GRATITUDE
1. Amy Morin, "7 Scientifically Proven Benefits of Gratitude That Will Motivate You to Give Thanks Year-Round," *Forbes*, November 23, 2014, https://www.forbes.com /sites/amymorin/2014/11/23/7-scientifically-proven-benefits-of-gratitude-that-will -motivate-you-to-give-thanks-year-round/#36bf4640183c.

GET MOVING
1. Ashish Sharma, Vishal Madaan, and Frederick D. Petty, "Exercise for Mental Health," *Primary Care Companion to the Journal of Clinical Psychiatry*, 8, no. 2, (2006):106, https://www.ncbi.nlm.nih.gov/pmc/articles/PMC1470658/.

TAKING PLAY SERIOUSLY
1. Marc Bekoff, "The Importance of Play: Having Fun Must Be Taken Seriously," *Psychology Today*, May 2, 2014, https://www.psychologytoday.com/us/blog/animal -emotions/201405/the-importance-play-having-fun-must-be-taken-seriously; Lawrence Robinson, Melinda Smith, Jeanne Segal, and Jennifer Shubin, "The Benefits of Play for Adults," HelpGuide.org, last updated March 2018, https://www .helpguide.org/articles/mental-health/benefits-of-play-for-adults.htm.

BREATHING DEEPLY
1. Mark Divine, "The Breathing Technique a Navy SEAL Uses to Stay Calm and Focused," *Motto*, May 4, 2016, http://time.com/4316151/breathing-technique-navy-seal-calm-focused/.

BITING MY TONGUE

1. Deane Alban, "Serotonin Deficiency: Signs, Symptoms, Solutions," *Be Brain Fit*, accessed January 11, 2018, https://bebrainfit.com/serotonin-deficiency/.

PROTECTING YOURSELF FROM THE CURSE OF COMPARISON

1. V. H. Medvec, S. F. Madey, and T. Gilovich, "When Less Is More: Counterfactual Thinking and Satisfaction Among Olympic Medalists, *Journal of Personality and Social Psychology*, October 1995, 69(4): 603–610, https://www.ncbi.nlm.nih.gov /pubmed/7473022.

GIVING FOR JOY

1. Amanda MacMillan, "Happiness: Being Generous Makes You Feel Better," *Time*, July 14, 2017, http://time.com/4857777/generosity-happiness-brain/.

GENEROSITY IS THE GIFT THAT KEEPS GIVING

1. Donald Moynihan, "Virtue Rewarded: Helping Others at Work Makes People Happier," *News: University of Wisconsin-Madison*, July 29, 2013, https://news.wisc .edu/virtue-rewarded-helping-others-at-work-makes-people-happier/.

INTENTIONAL SOCIAL MEDIA

1. Holly B. Shakya and Nicholas A. Christakis, "Association of Facebook Use with Compromised Well-Being: A Longitudinal Study," *American Journal of Epidemiology* 185, issue 3 (February 1, 2017): 203–211, https://doi.org/10.1093 /aje/kww189; Niraj Chokshi, "Want to Be Happy? Buy More Takeout and Hire a Maid, Study Suggests," *New York Times*, July 27, 2017, https://www.nytimes .com/2017/07/27/science/study-happy-save-money-time.html.

DELEGATING THE DRUDGERY

1. Chokshi, Niraj. "Want to Be Happy? Buy More Takeout and Hire a Maid, Study Suggests," *New York Times*, July 27, 2017. Accessed January 14, 2018, https://www .nytimes.com/2017/07/27/science/study-happy-save-money-time.html.

ABOUT THE AUTHOR

Hi, friends. I'm Alli. My husband Mark and I live outside of Nashville with our five sons and the only golden retriever who refuses to retrieve. I am passionate about sharing the truth and love of God while providing practical tools we can use to live the life we are created to live.

I write books about my journey and the lessons I've learned. *Breaking Busy* was written to help us all have a road map to live with purpose and happiness instead of busyness and pressure. *Fierce Faith* is a battle plan to help women fight fear, wrestle worry, and overcome anxiety.

You can join me weekly on *The Alli Worthington Show*, a weekly podcast where I get to interview and learn from brilliant people and even do some fun coaching. I would love for you to join in and have a listen.

xo,

Alli

LET'S STAY FRIENDS!

What a journey of happiness it has been. Thank you for joining in. We are part of a group of thousands of women seeking holy happiness, fighting for our joy, and walking in truth. The next step is to be sure to be in community with like-minded women, find our battle buddies, and keep growing.

I would love for you to join us in the Women of Fierce Faith Community where we seek what is good, celebrate each other, and most of all, work to glorify Jesus.

You can go to my website at AlliWorthington.com to join in the fun!